822.33
D71s

134974

DATE DUE			

The Swan at the Well

The wan at the Well

Shakespeare
Reading
Chaucer

E. Talbot Donaldson

Yale University Press
New Haven and London

Designed by Nancy Ovedovitz, and set in Linotron 202
Bembo type, by Graphic Composition Inc., Athens,
Georgia. Printed in the United States of America by
Edwards Brothers Inc., Ann Arbor, Michigan.

Library of Congress Cataloging in Publication Data
Donaldson, E. Talbot (Ethelbert Talbot), 1910–
    The swan at the well.
    Bibliography: p.
    Includes index.
    1. Shakespeare, William, 1564–1616—Sources. 2. Chaucer,
Geoffrey, d. 1400—Influence—Shakespeare. I. Title.
PR2955.C53D6 1985   822.3'3   84-21913
ISBN 0-300-03349-4 (alk. paper)

The paper in this book meets the guidelines for permanence
and durability of the Committee on Production Guidelines
for Book Longevity of the Council on Library Resources.

10 9 8 7 6 5 4 3 2 1

For Judith

Contents

Acknowledgments

 number of benefactors have helped me in the completion of this book, and I am deeply grateful to them all: first, the President and faculty in English at Bryn Mawr College for inviting me to serve as the Mary Flexner Lecturer in the autumn of 1981; the chapters of the present book were in their original form those lectures. For the hospitality that my wife and I received at Bryn Mawr we both thank our many friends there; it was a delightful situation in which to spend the autumn and we have the fondest memories of our stay. To the John Simon Guggenheim Memorial Foundation I am indebted for a fellowship for the academic year 1977–78, when I first began to work actively on the topic of Chaucer and Shakespeare, which had been in the back of my mind for many years. I am indebted too to the Fellows and the staff of the Huntington Library, which granted me a stipend for three months in 1982, and where I was treated most hospitably as a reader during the first half of 1978: the Huntington is truly a paradise for scholars. The National Endowment for the Humanities appointed me Director of a Summer Seminar given at Bloomington on the subject of Chaucer and Shakespeare in 1977, and asked me to repeat the Seminar in 1980. I am most grateful for the opportunities these seminars offered me to think further on the subject and to discuss it with two lively groups of college teachers whom I found enormously stimulating.

I should note here that the book of essays that resulted from my second seminar, edited by Judith J. Kollmann and myself, is not mentioned in this volume except on one occasion: *Chaucer-*

ian Shakespeare: Adaptation and Transformation, Medieval and Renaissance Monograph Series II (Detroit: Michigan Consortium for Medieval and Early Modern Studies, 1983). The editing of these essays fell in the middle of my own work—in several senses—and since they are all, so to speak, within the family, I decided not to refer to them in my own text, but to recommend to the reader here those that are concerned with specific topics touched on in my book: for *A Midsummer Night's Dream* the articles by Valerie S. Roberts and James Spisak; and for the Wife of Bath and Falstaff, those by Laurie A. Finke and Nancy T. Leslie. The Wife of Bath is considered in another Shakespearean context, *The Taming of the Shrew*, by Sr. Frances Gussenhoven, RSHM. I find the ideas in these essays highly congenial, and I can only hope that their authors derived some measure of compensation from my tutelage for any of their insights that I have inadvertently appropriated. I am sure that my debt to the other members of this seminar, as well as to the members of the earlier one in 1977, is equally real if undeterminable. The only essay in the 1983 volume that I refer to in my text is Judith Kollmann's on the similarity of the social milieu of *The Merry Wives of Windsor* to that of *The Canterbury Tales*: this is something I simply had not noticed. I also recommend to the reader the highly adventurous articles by Thomas Moisan and Carol Shilkett, who explore possible Chaucerian influences on Shakespeare in contexts with no tangible Chaucerian background: I hope that in the future there will be more such imaginative studies.

Of the many friends with whom I have discussed matters in this book I single out for special thanks Liz and Dan Donno and Catherine Shaw from the Huntington days, and Joe Kramer at Bryn Mawr; they may none of them realize how much their passing comments have helped me. For assistance with certain references I thank Sara Hanna and Imtiaz Habib at Indiana University. My greatest debt is to the person to whom this book is dedicated. She encouraged me to continue work on it when, in 1979, a consciousness of failing health combined with the appearance of Ann Thompson's *Shakespeare's Chaucer* (1978) made me contemplate abandoning the project. This is Judith Anderson's book in more ways than one.

Introduction

he chapters of this book treat the plays of Shakespeare that are most indebted to works by Chaucer. *A Midsummer Night's Dream*, which I take up first, bears a strong relation to *The Knight's Tale* and, in a lesser degree, to three other Chaucerian works: *The Merchant's Tale, The Tale of Sir Thopas*, and the story of Pyramus and Thisbe as it is told in *The Legend of Good Women*. The titular heroes of *The Two Noble Kinsmen* are, of course, the two young knights of *The Knight's Tale*, and the lovers of *Troilus and Cressida* are the descendants of those of Chaucer's *Troilus and Criseyde*. After considering these relationships I discuss, more conjecturally, the possible influence of *Troilus and Criseyde* on *Romeo and Juliet*, and of the Wife of Bath on the conception of Falstaff.

These specific relations have of course been discussed before, and there have been occasional broader considerations of Shakespeare's relation to Chaucer: one thinks first perhaps of the early (and excellent) unsigned article in the *Quarterly Review* in 1873, generally assigned to J. W. Hales,[1] and there is the more recent (and disappointing) contribution of Nevill Coghill to the festschrift for F. P. Wilson in 1959.[2] And now there is Ann Thompson's book (1978), which covers the whole field of Chaucer and Shakespeare with considerable care.[3]

Yet these general comparative studies, and many, many more on individual plays (especially *Troilus*) do not, on the whole, do justice to the relationship. Many of the earlier ones are primarily concerned with gathering points of similarity or echoes to prove that Shakespeare read Chaucer, and they have little to say about larger relationships. But comparisons more recent, made since Shakespeare's knowledge has become (more or less generally) accepted, also often seem deficient. This results, I fear, from the fact that, with the exception of Coghill, most critics concerned with comparisons have been primarily Shakespeareans and only incidentally Chaucerians; I believe this is true even of Ann Thompson. Shakespeareans are naturally interested in showing how the Chaucerian background can illuminate the plays, but this perfectly proper interest often has the effect of assuming that, although the play is a puzzle requiring answers, the Chaucerian works that may help provide answers have settled—one might almost say static—meanings that are available to any reader. To one who has spent much of his scholarly life trying to unravel Chaucerian meanings this assumption represents a serious misunderstanding of a poet of enormous complexity and subtlety, whose meanings are apt to be as many-faceted and as various as Shakespeare's. The Chaucer the comparativist critics discuss often seems to me remote and even secondhand. Sometimes I find it hard to recognize the poem the critic is referring to as the one by Chaucer that I know; at other times I recognize it as an interpretation of the poem once widely current but now subject to serious challenge, if not wholly discredited. A comparison based on the assumption that Chaucer meant but one thing to Shakespeare and did not offer him the complexities that he offers modern readers cannot hope to attain much depth. My essays are the result of my discontent with the shallowness of the majority—though, to be sure, not all—of the comparisons that have been made. Shakespeare himself provides the final indication of the way Shakespeare read Chaucer, and that way is with full appreciation of his complexity.

The Chaucerian background of *A Midsummer Night's Dream* is a case in point. Although an excellent start on considering the wider implications of Shakespeare's use of Chaucer was made by Dorothy Bethurum in 1945,[4] discussions since then have usually been limited, rather anachronistically, to matters of detail, to echoes which, though confirming Shakespeare's debt to Chaucer, tell us nothing of real interest about how his imagination responded to and refashioned Chaucer's art. The serene

skepticism, not to say cynicism, of which Chaucer is every-
where capable and which has made its way into Shakespeare's
play has hardly been noted amid the welter of small borrowings,
and poor Sir Thopas' baleful influence on the artisans' play has
gone almost unrecognized. Even Ann Thompson seems to lose
her usual shrewdness with *A Midsummer Night's Dream*, and her
discussion of it is one of the few disappointing parts of her
book. I hope my chapters add to an understanding of how
Chaucer and Shakespeare handled—in this case in rather similar
ways—human folly and its frequent corollary, artistic absurdity.

With *The Two Noble Kinsmen* in relation to *The Knight's Tale* I
must withdraw my complaint that Shakespeareans show inadequate knowledge of Chaucer. Philip Edwards' discussion of the
two works (along with Clifford Leech's shorter one) manifests
an understanding of *The Knight's Tale* that is richer than that of
some Chaucerians.[5] Ann Thompson has also written well on
this topic, but I consider Edwards' article a model of what comparative criticism can be. What I have to offer here is therefore
augmentation of his theme: he sees Venus as the principal dis-
rupter of human life in both Chaucer's poem and in the play,
and I see Mars as an equally disruptive force, rather implicit in
Chaucer but explicit in Shakespeare. My comparison also results in a Theseus in Shakespeare who has even less justification
than Chaucer's Theseus for asserting the existence of a principle
of divine justice that neither work sanctions.

It is with *Troilus and Cressida* that an inadequate understanding
of what Chaucer wrote in *Troilus and Criseyde* is most damaging
to any discussion of the two works—and sometimes damaging
to the meaning of both. It is my conviction, based on a mass of
evidence, that Shakespeare understood Chaucer's poem for
what it is, a marvelous celebration of romantic love containing
a sad recognition of its fragility, a work full of ironic contradic-
tions and yet ringing true in a way that far more realistic literature fails to do. But the poem one often meets in the criticism
of Shakespeare's play is one with a relatively straightforward,
oversimplified meaning, and a meaning that is more often im-
plied by the critic than stated. Frequently one recognizes the
presence in the critic's mind of C. S. Lewis's famous reading of

the poem in *The Allegory of Love*,[6] an interpretation as brilliant as it has been influential, and in my opinion one that fails wholly to accord with Shakespeare's apparent understanding of the poem. Chaucerian critics have in the last quarter-century provided more than one alternative to Lewis's interpretation, and alternatives that far better correspond to Shakespeare's own understanding of the poem: one of these—my own—is the basis for my criticism in this book. Surprisingly, I do not remember seeing any of these alternative interpretations cited by Shakespearean critics discussing the play. Indeed, it is something of a curiosity that Chaucerian critics, aside from Lewis, are rarely cited in such discussions. Even Ann Thompson, who has a very wide knowledge of Chaucer, betrays her Shakespearean bias by rarely citing any but Shakespearean critics.

My conclusions depend on the assumption that Shakespeare read Chaucer's poetry with understanding and great care, more carefully, perhaps, than some of his critics. One eminent Shakespearean—an excellent critic usually—tells us that Chaucer's Pandarus is "younger" than Shakespeare's, when actually Chaucer's Pandarus is of wholly indeterminate age: students' estimates of his age are apt to vary by as many as forty years.[7] This critic's may seem a minor error, hardly worth noting; and so too when he tells us that Chaucer's Diomede is a more respectable person than his Shakespearean counterpart.[8] But the first error suggests that the critic has failed to realize that Chaucer's poem is a vast assemblage of unknowns, of half-truths and half-perceptions on which each must build his understanding of the poem—something Shakespeare did not miss. The three characters we know best are all to a large extent mysterious, and among the things we don't know about them is the age of any one of them, any more than Chaucer's narrator knows whether or not Criseyde had any children by her deceased husband. And looked at carefully Chaucer's Diomede is as caddish a cad as Shakespeare's, if a shade less "sudden," to use Chaucer's word for him. The suggestion that Chaucer's Diomede is more gentlemanly than Shakespeare's logically implies a system that makes Criseyde's behavior less whorish than Cressida's (though the critic I am citing does not, I think, pursue this implication).

Cressida has been the target of vilification based on her presumed deterioration since the time she was Criseyde. My two
chapters on the poem and play suggest that Shakespeare naturally understood the ambiguity with which the poem had
treated Criseyde, and that he implanted in Cressida a complex
ambiguity of her own. On the other hand, critics have assumed
too much similarity between the two Troiluses, and have failed
to observe how unsatisfactory a lover Shakespeare's is, with the
result that Cressida is made to seem guilty of betraying the
much more gentlemanly Troilus of Chaucer's poem rather than
the dedicated solipsist of Shakespeare's play.

In the works I have been discussing the Chaucerian poems
serve as a kind of substructure for the Shakespearean plays. But
Troilus and Criseyde and the Wife of Bath in their relation respectively to *Romeo and Juliet* and Falstaff seem better described as
infrastructures: if they do not serve as the foundation on which
Shakespeare built, they do seem to provide some of the important ways and means by which he was enabled to build as he
did. That they are not part of the same structure is suggested by
the lack of verbal echoes—and even echoes less narrowly defined—in what Shakespeare created; yet though the lack of such
echoes is considered technically fatal to establishing influence,
the fact remains that one work may be strongly influenced by
another without ever repeating a single phrase or word from it:
borrowers do not always leave fingerprints by which they may
be detected, and totally efficient assimilators devour their sub-
structures. A discussion of the similarities betweeen the earlier
and the later can be revealing to both even if it fails to prove
borrowing; and if the similarities are sufficiently impressive despite the absence of echoes the argument for influence becomes
less questionable: indeed, I rather imagine that some day it will
be a matter of general belief that the two greatest love poems in
English, like the two greatest comic characters, are closely related. I hope that my discussion will provide some impetus toward this belief.

Comparative criticism such as I conduct here, between the
greatest of literary artists and one only a little less great, is so
large a pleasure that I feel almost self-indulgent in practicing it.

Yet the fact is that both Chaucer and Shakespeare were enter-
tainers who brought pleasure to their auditors. And because the
exercise of the imagination in producing fictional worlds is one
of the most pleasing of its uses (and through fictional worlds we
comprehend what is real), the use of our imaginations in comparing the fictional worlds of two supreme creators should
rightly be pure pleasure. Fortunately, not all comparisons have
to be odious. I hope the reader may share the enjoyment that I
have felt in making the comparisons in this book.

I

The Embarrassments of Art:
The Tale of Sir Thopas,
"Pyramus and Thisbe," and
A Midsummer Night's Dream

hen in the *Canterbury Tales* the unnamed narrator of the pilgrimage—presumably someone called Geoffrey—is summarily ordered by the Host to tell a tale, he responds apologetically. He hopes the Host will not be ill-pleased,

> For other tale certes can I none
> But of a rime I lerned yore agone.   [B² 1898–99]¹

Yet his face reflects the anticipatory pleasure he feels at the thought of retelling the old rhyme he learned long ago—the sole bit of literary lumber in the storehouse of his memory—and the Host interprets this pleased expression as a promise that the pilgrims are about to hear "som deinte thing," a delightful story. Thus encouraged, the narrator launches into the story of Sir Thopas, which turns out to be a chivalric romance consisting largely of narrative clichés imprisoned in one of the most relentless meters one could grind out with the aid of a metronome:

> Listeneth, lordinges, in good intent,
> And I wol tell verament
>   Of Mirthe and of solas;
> All of a knight was faire and gent
> In batayle and in turnament:
>   His name was sir Thopas.   [B² 1902–07]

And so on for 206 inexorable lines describing the non-adventures of an unusually uninteresting knight. At the two hundred and seventh line the Host can no longer contain his fury at having been so deceived in his expectation, and it bursts forth:

> "NO more of this, for Goddes dignite,"
> Quod our hoste, "for thou makest me
> So wery of thy very leudenes
> That also wisly God my soule blesse
> Mine eares aken of thy drastie speache.
> Now soche a rime the devill I beteache.
> This maie well be clepe rime Dogrell," quod he.
> "Why so?" quod I. "Why wolt thou let me
> More of my tale than any other man,
> Sens that it is the best rime I can?"
> "By god," quod he, "plainly, at o worde,
> Thy drastie riming is not worthe a torde.
> Thou doest nought else but spendest time.
> Sir, at one worde, thou shalt no lenger rime."   [B² 2109–22]

It is well known that Chaucer's *Tale of Sir Thopas* is a superlative parody of all the worst features of the worst kind of Middle English romance, a masterpiece of deconstructive criticism. But its status as a parody wholly escapes its narrator, as it wholly escapes the Host. It remains for the pilgrim "the best rime I can," the best poem he knows, and a serious endeavor of art. This narrator is the stand-in, the shadow, of the greatest narrative poet in English; and he reveals, by his injured innocence, by his unawareness of having committed any artistic offense, the wry recognition of his creator Chaucer that, viewed with a certain hardheadedness, the difference between the best and the worst in the fiction-making kind is but small: all narratives are only distant imitations of reality, so that if a narrator proceeds according to the time-honored rules for creating fiction, as both Chaucer and his surrogate narrator do, what more can one ask? A good black-and-white photograph and a bad one are alike in being merely light and shadow on paper. But the Host is not interested in the finer points of criticism: he knows a bad verse story when he hears one and sentences the pilgrim to prose for his second attempt.

The narrator's question, "Why do you stop me from telling the best story I know when you let others go on?" receives a somewhat more sympathetic answer—though not a very sympathetic one—from another character in the *Canterbury Tales*, Duke Theseus of Athens; this answer is not, however, given until after Theseus' transfer from Chaucer's *Knight's Tale* to Shakespeare's *A Midsummer Night's Dream*. Speaking of another serious endeavor of art, Peter Quince's play of "Pyramus and Thisbe," Theseus' bride, Hippolyta, remarks, "This is the silliest stuff that ever I heard" (V.i.207). To this Theseus replies, with perhaps both more and less appreciation for the difficulty art has in imitating nature, "The best in this kind are but shadows; and the worst are no worse, if imagination amend them"[2]—whether it is the artist's imagination or, as Hipppolyta suggests it must be with "Pyramus and Thisbe," the audience's.

Although the Chaucerian elements in *A Midsummer Night's Dream* have long been recognized (and, curiously enough, sometimes been belittled), that the play of Pyramus is the moral equivalent—an inspired re-creation—of Chaucer's *Tale of Sir Thopas* has not been generally noticed, though it was hinted at many years ago by G. K. Chesterton. Discussing the irony of Chaucer's assignment to his own surrogate of the worst tale told on the Canterbury pilgrimage, Chesterton quotes Theseus' "The best in this kind are but shadows," but then moves away from the Shakespearean connection.[3] Even Dorothy Bethurum in her thorough article on Chaucerian themes in *A Midsummer Night's Dream* seems to have missed the relation to *Sir Thopas* of the Pyramus play, though it was she who first pointed out that Shakespeare actually awarded to Bottom the elf-queen that Chaucer's Sir Thopas only dreamed of possessing[4] (one of Sir Thopas' typically inert adventures is lying on the soft grass and vowing to love no woman but an elf-queen). But there are larger connections between the burlesque romance and the burlesque play. In either case, a master of a literary form makes fun of old-fashioned and primitive examples of that form while he is himself engaged in writing in it, and then assigns his parody to the most naive and most naively self-confident of artists. Yet at the same time that each is asserting by example his superiority in the form, he acknowledges that his own art—or all art—may be equally insubstantial, equally absurd. For all art relies as confidently and in a way as naively on certain conventions as Peter Quince and his associates do and as Chaucer the pilgrim does. It is true that Geoffrey and Peter assume in the reader or onlooker an involuntary and overwhelming suspension of disbelief, but the difference between their assumptions and those of better artists is only a matter of degree. The parody of the worst poems and of the worst plays cannot help but be in some respects a parody of the best.

In what ways *Sir Thopas* is a perfect parody of the Middle English tail-rhyme romance has been most exhaustively demonstrated by Laura Hibbard Loomis.[5] In what ways and of what works the play "Pyramus and Thisbe" is a parody has received even more consideration. It is interesting that whereas some pre-Shakespearean dramas, such as *Cambises* and Jaspar Heywood's *Hercules Furens*, have been identified as sources of the artisans' play, a number of other suggested sources are not bad plays but bad poems: this perhaps tends to confirm the influence of *Sir Thopas*. But of course the rhetorical excesses are the same in bad verse drama and in bad verse narrative; nor do I intend here to propose *Sir Thopas* as a substitute for any of the works that Kenneth Muir and others have suggested as sources for "Pyramus and Thisbe": I should merely like to add it to the list.[6] I note, however, that one of Muir's most prominent candidates, Thomas Mouffet's poem *Of the Silkewormes, and their Flies*, has recently been vigorously challenged,[7] and if Mouffet is disqualified, I should be happy to see Sir Thopas take his place. Besides, *Sir Thopas* does have a thematic relation to "Pyramus and Thisbe" that none of the others can claim.

The relation extends to matters of detail. Both parodies recognize that the logic of poetry and the logic of everyday common sense are not at all the same thing, but bad poets confuse the two. "Sun" may remind anyone of "moon" because both give light, but a good poet's imagination is alert to the difference in kind and quality. Not so the author of *Sir Thopas* describing his hero's radiant armament:

> His bridle as the Sunne shone,
>   Or as the Moone light.   [B² 2069–70]

As twin gods, Apollo and Diana deserve, as it were, equal time, and the author courteously if inaccurately awards Diana a luminescence equal to Apollo's. Quince's Pyramus is equally courteous in returning the compliment by reversing the image:

> Sweet Moon, I thank thee for thy sunny beams.   [V.i.261]

Similarly, a strict sense of justice—non-poetic justice—may cause an amateur poet to misuse conventions. Middle English poetry had certain well-established conventions for describing the physical attributes of females, and it had others for males. But since males and females do share certain physical attributes, a writer influenced by considerations of justice may reverse the accepted imagery, thus endangering the sexual integrity of the person described. Heroines of Middle English romance are ordinarily distinguished for their peaches-and-cream complexions, whereas the complexions of heroes are either hidden by beards or unmentioned. But young men sometimes have as nice complexions as their beloveds, and the narrator of *Sir Thopas* feels it only fair to mention his hero's approximation of peaches-and-cream:

> White was his face as paine maine,
>   His lippes reed as rose.
> His rudde is like scarlet in graine.   [B² 1915–17]

Thisbe's description of Pyramus in the rehearsal of their play—the passage was apparently cut out before opening night—almost outdoes Chaucer's description of Sir Thopas in the process of demasculinization:

> Most radiant Pyramus, most lily-white of hue,
> Of colour like the red rose on triumphant briar.   [III.i.88–89]

Actually, Shakespeare's image gains some of its ludicrousness from the fact that the word Chaucer used, *rode* (rudde), meaning

the peaches, or at least the red, in the peaches-and-cream combination, had fallen out of usage except in the generalized adjec-
tival form "ruddy." That is, Sir Thopas' face was as white as the
finest white bread, except for his *rode*, presumably his cheeks
and lips, which were like, respectively, deep-died cloth of scarlet
and red roses: he might have looked like a clown to us, but to
his chronicler he was as pretty as any heroine. Poor Pyramus,
on the other hand, is at once lily-white of hue and rose red of
color, with no anatomical boundaries separating the two—an
eye-catching anomaly, if a splotchy one.

Neither Chaucer nor Shakespeare was one to let a good joke
die after only one epiphany. Later in the tale, Chaucer mentions
Sir Thopas' "sides smale" (B^2 1026), slender flanks that form the
dainty shape which is usually reserved exclusively for delicate
damsels. Similarly, Pyramus committing suicide directs his
sword to "that left pap / Where heart doth hop," thereby
preempting a bit of the anatomy more generally, if not univer-
sally, considered a female property.[8] In her lamentation over her
dead lover, Thisbe lavishes on him a number of epithets suggesting that she and he would have made good modern unisex
lovers, hard to tell apart:

> These lily lips,
> This cherry nose,
> These yellow cowslip cheeks,
> Are gone, are gone!   [V.i.317–20]

The lilies and cherries are, by long tradition, part of her own
fair femininity, but here she generously assigns them to Pyramus—though with a physiognomical misplacement by which
the lips become white and the nose red. I'm uncertain of the
rhetorical gender of yellow cowslip cheeks or eyes as green as
leeks that Thisbe also ascribes to Pyramus:[9] perhaps they are
produced by a democratic wish to give as much poetic credit to
lesser forms of vegetation like cowslips and leeks as to the somewhat over-publicized roses and lilies.

In respect to hair, however, Sir Thopas at least is very masculine:

His heer, his berde was like safroun
　　That to his girdel raught adoun.   [B² 1920–21]

This bright saffron bushiness may have influenced Bottom's consideration of the appropriate beard to assume for the role of Pyramus:

> I will discharge it in either your straw-colour beard, your orange-tawny ǀ beard, ǀ your ǀ purple-in-grain beard, or your French-crown-colour beard, your perfect yellow.   [I.ii.86–89]

Muir notes that Mouffet's poem on silkworms has *orange* and *tawny* in successive lines,[10] but there the colors do not refer to beards, but to moths of a different color from the silkworms. I suspect Bottom is leaning toward the orange-red or orange-yellow of Sir Thopas' saffron beard for Pyramus', and that the possible alternative of purple-in-grain may have been suggested by the scarlet-in-grain *rudde* of Sir Thopas. One wonders how much of Sir Thopas' lovely complexion was visible beneath or behind saffron beard and hair reaching to his waistline: one doubts that Bottom would hide his light under so large a bushel.

The otiosity of tail-rhyme romance and of the rhetoric of early drama often results from the poet's desperate need for a rhyme, or else from his willingness to settle for the first one that comes along. In neither Middle nor Elizabethan English is the rhyme *-ain* a hard one, but the word *certaín*, with the stress wrenched to the second syllable, often appears in rhyme in lesser poets of both eras, faute de mieux. The result is apt to be an earnest asseveration of a fact not really subject to dispute, as when the narrator, needing a rhyme for *grain*, remarks of Sir Thopas:

And I you tell in good certaine
　　He had a semely nose;   [B² 1918–19]

or the result may be an emphatic revelation of the obvious, as in Quince's Prologue's announcement, when he needs a rhyme for *plain*,

This beauteous lady Thisbe is certain.   [V.i.129]

Thisbe's identity, if not her beauteousness, is hardly open to question. Muir notes that *certaín* occurs, inevitably, in one of the Pyramus poems Shakespeare probably knew, that of J. Thomson in *A Handfull of Pleasant Delites*.[11] But it was surely not J. Thomson that Shakespeare was making fun of, but—like Chaucer—all the lazy versifiers who reject rhyme's challenge to make them think.

Unresourceful poets were also accustomed to eke out their lines with an *eke*. Thus Sir Thopas is made to swear an oath "By dale and eke by doune" to love only an elf-queen (B² 1986): it seems curious to swear by valleys and hills, but it is clear from the *eke* that to the formulation of Sir Thopas' high resolve the contingent downs are every bit as essential as the dales. In the rehearsal scene of the Pyramus play Thisbe refers to her lover as a

> Most brisky juvenal, and eke most lovely Jew.   [III.i.90]

Here the Roman satirist is confused with a young man (for neither the first nor the last time), and *Jew* is evidently thought to be a short form of *juvenile*, the relationship being reinforced by the *eke*. Muir suggests that Shakespeare is here making fun of Mouffet's practice of using *eke* as metrical filler;[12] but I suspect that Shakespeare had no particular poet in mind but all poetic ekers out, including, perhaps, Chaucer—who may also have had Chaucer in mind when he used seven very idle *ekes* in the short space of *Sir Thopas'* two-hundred-odd lines; though this combined density and otiosity of *ekes* is not matched elsewhere in Chaucer, *eke* is nevertheless so common in him that the Chaucer *Concordance* lists only specimens. In all of Shakespeare's works, on the other hand, there are only two adverbial *ekes* besides the present one:[13] of Shakespeare's many remarkable achievements, this almost total abstention from *eke* seems to me not the least remarkable.

Though Shakespeare's Pyramus play has no clear example of that most idle of rhetorical figures, *correctio* (not this, but that, as when Sir Thopas' spear "biddeth warre & nothing pees" [B² 2072]), Pyramus does invoke the similar poetic privilege of extending an image beyond the immediate requirements of the context. He addresses night,

> O grim-look'd night! O night with hue so black!
> O night, which ever art when day is not!   [V.i.168–69]

Pyramus' understandable attempt to find something in night to comment on besides its darkness proves, unfortunately, abortive, with the result that he seems to be doing what the Host accuses *Sir Thopas'* narrator of doing, merely wasting time. But the observation that night always exists in the absence of day is not wholly unlike another, more serious observation made elsewhere in Shakespeare, about sleep:

>   the innocent sleep,
> Sleep that knits up the ravell'd sleave of care,
> The death of each day's life, sore labor's bath,
> Balm of hurt minds, great nature's second course,
> Chief nourisher in life's feast.   [II.ii.33–37]

Macbeth hath murdered sleep, but not the poetic images of its healing functions, which live on to haunt his imagination. Lady Macbeth's interruption of her husband's ill-timed meditation on sleep, "What do you mean?" is an attempt to pull him out of an attack of poetical rhetoric so severe as to bring the action of the play to a halt: his speech is, from her point of view, nothing but a waste of valuable time. Indeed, Macbeth's immediate audience, his wife, is as impatient as Pyramus' audience is of the attempt to do rhetorical justice to the dramatic situation.

A striking feature of the play of Pyramus is the actors', especially Bottom's, overconfidence in the power of their art. They fear that their verisimilitude will be such that the audience will be unable to distinguish their performance from reality. Therefore, in order to counteract that, a lion must roar as gently as any sucking dove, as Bottom brags he can, or else it must carefully explain that it is Snug the joiner, who is "a lion fell, nor else no lion's dam" (V.i.219)—apparently a lion in skin only. Without this abjuration of leoninity, the ladies in the audience might be frightened by the lion, which, according to Prologue,

"Did scare away, or rather did affright" (V.i.140) poor Thisbe. Perhaps "scare away, or rather . . . affright" should be considered an example of *correctio*, but it is a curious example because the contrast between "scare away" and "affright" exists nowhere but in the speaker's mind. Possibly he thought it more ladylike to be affrighted than to be scared away.

Chaucer's narrator is as careful as the artisans are not to distress his audience unnecessarily. The giant who challenges Sir Thopas in Fairyland is not assigned three heads until after Sir Thopas has safely escaped from him: it might be too much for a sensitive reader to witness Sir Thopas having stones slung at him by a three-headed Goliath. And lest the reader find the suspense of the hero's impending adventure intolerable, the poet mitigates it:

> He pricketh through a faire forest:
> Therein was many a wilde beest,
>   Ye, bothe Bucke and Hare.
> And as he pricketh Northe and Este,
> I tell you, him hadde almeste
>   Betide a sorie care. [B² 1944–49]

Those who shudder at the prospect of Sir Thopas' being bitten by a wild buck or an attack-rabbit are reassured that what is to come, though a near thing, will not be fatal—Sir Thopas almost, but not quite, had a sorry care betide him. This is a most courteous *almost*, and of a good conscience. Indeed, Chaucer's and Shakespeare's parodies are alike in the comfortable motherliness of their solicitude for the audience's peace of mind, even if, in the case of Bottom and his friends, it is tinged with prudence in their not wanting to scare away, or rather affright, the ladies.

Just before lying down to rest and to dedicate himself to the task of finding an elf-queen to be his mistress, Sir Thopas is treated to an avian concert in the forest:

> The briddes singen, it is no naie,
> The Sperhauke and the Popingaie,
>   That ioie it was to here.
> The Throstell eke made his laie;

> The wodcoke vpon the spraie,
>   She song full loude and clere.   [B² 1956–61]

When Bottom's fellow-actors find him wearing an ass's head and run away, he keeps up his courage by singing a song about birds, little suspecting that he is being overheard by the very elf-queen Sir Thopas has vowed to find:

> The ousel cock, so black of hue,
> With orange-tawny bill [Bottom's favorite color],
> The throstle, with his note so true,
>   The wren with little quill—   [III.i.120–23]

and soon the unseen Titania rouses herself to inquire, "What angel wakes me from my flowery bed?" The birdsong Sir Thopas hears would in any medieval romance be provided to a hero with love on his mind wandering through the woods, though without, one hopes, the squawk and squeak of parrot and sparrowhawk; but the concert has become more functional in Shakespeare—if in a manner somewhat askew—because the birds are framed within a human song that incites an elf-queen to amorous aggression. Not birdsong but singing about birds gets Bottom a fairy mistress.

It is interesting that Shakespeare's respect for Bottom was too great to allow him to imitate Sir Thopas' narrator's ignorance of birdsongs: Bottom knew that the song of the sparrowhawk was nothing to sing about, nor was the song of the parrot—the popinjay—which in Bottom's time no longer infested the woods of England (or of Athens) as it had been permitted to do by the writers of Middle English romance. Bottom's birds are all genuine songbirds, whereas the throstle (the song thrush) is the only real songbird on Sir Thopas' list.[14] But for Chaucer's unnatural natural history Shakespeare substitutes Bottom's classification of your lion as an *avis*, the most fearful of wild-fowl, and of your sucking dove, obviously, as a mammal.

As the temperature of the action in the story of Sir Thopas rises, the verse form changes, either to accommodate the rise or, because the rise is minimal, to indicate that there is one. The first thirteen stanzas are all admirably if murderously regular tail-rhyme, $a = a = b = a = a = b$, with the tetrametric a–lines and the trimetric *b*–lines. But as the excitement mounts (or stirs in its sleep) with Thopas' vow to find an elf-queen to sleep under his gore, an extra pair of *c*–lines appears, and the stanza form suffers some elegant variation before settling down to strict regularity before the poem's untimely termination. Peter Quince's play is written mainly in pentameter lines with alternating rhymes or else in couplets, but when the tragic climax approaches and Pyramus finds Thisbe's mantle slain, the verse accelerates into the form of eight-and-six with internal rhyme. Muir points out that this is the form of Thomson's Pyramus poem, from which Muir thinks Shakespeare probably got it.[15] But it is perhaps worth noting that eight-and-six is kin to tail-rhyme, which is eight-eight-and-six without internal rhyme: certain verse forms make natural vehicles for extravagantly bad poetry. And just as the author of *Sir Thopas* began to have trouble finding four *a*–rhymes per stanza and so settles for two pairs, rhyme also eludes Peter Quince at one point during Thisbe's lament (V.i.317–18), and he settles by pairing *lips* with *nose*, a far cry even from assonance.

Quince's play itself is generally acknowledged to be in part the result of Shakespeare's reading of the translation by Golding of Ovid's *Metamorphoses*, though Shakespeare must have known Ovid as well. But most modern scholars allow that Shakespeare was influenced by Chaucer's retelling of the story of Pyramus and Thisbe in *The Legend of Good Women*; the Chaucerian connection is reinforced by the fact that the lion-crossed lovers are alluded to in Chaucer's *Merchant's Tale*, which left its mark in other ways on *A Midsummer Night's Dream*. Like Chaucer, Shakespeare omits the metamorphosis of the mulberry leaves and hence also omits the mulberry tree (though Chaucer does mention an unidentified tree). It was Chaucer, as a future Clerk of the Works preoccupied with technical matters, who first became interested in the exact composition of the wall that separated Pyramus' parents' house from Thisbe's. In Ovid and Golding this is only an old wall with a chink in it. But in Chaucer, in their joint address to the wall, after first calling it wicked,[16] the lovers thank it,

In as muche as thou suffrest for to gone
Our wordes through thy lime & eke thy stone.   [764–65]

This splendid *eke* displays the lovers' knowledge of what goes
into a wall—lime and *also* stone: no straw without bricks in
Babylon. Shakespeare scarcely needed Chaucer to tell him about
the composition of house walls, but he follows his lead in referring to Wall in terms of the synecdoches of its constructional
components. When Quince first realizes that Wall must be included in the play's Cast of Characters, Bottom suggests that
the part be played by a man with "some plaster, or some loam,
or some rough-cast [lime and gravel] about him" (III.i.64–65).
Prologue identifies Wall as consisting of lime and rough-cast
(V.i.130), and Wall catalogues his own constituents as "This
loam, this rough-cast, and this stone" (160). Theseus continues
the inventory by inquiring, after Wall's self-introduction,
"Would you desire lime and hair to speak better?" (164). Pyramus, unable to spy Thisbe through Wall's usually cooperative
chink, reduces the structure to its primary element when he
cries, rather unfairly and illogically,

O wicked wall, through whom I see no bliss,
Curs'd be thy stones for thus deceiving me!   [178–79]

Finally Thisbe, approaching Wall's opposite face, gives it a more
ample and accurate description when she remarks that her
cherry lips

have often kiss'd thy stones,
Thy stones with lime and hair knit up in thee.   [188–89]

Would you desire a wall to be defined better?

Another detail in Shakespeare's parody play may have been
suggested by Chaucer's *Legend*: Moonshine's exit after Pyramus
has stabbed himself but before Thisbe finds his body. In Ovid
(and Golding) moonlight is mentioned only once, when by it
Thisbe sees the lioness from afar; presumably the moon went
on shining through the subsequent action at Ninus' tomb.
Chaucer, who was sporadically scrupulous about keeping the
minutiae of his stories consistent, adds the matter of the moon's

aid to Pyramus in spotting the lioness's footprints and the bloody wimple—and Shakespeare's Pyramus politely thanks Moonshine for the help of his sunny beams just before he makes his awful discovery of Thisbe's mantle. But Chaucer fails to mention the moon as helping Thisbe spy her lover's body, allowing it to exit, as it were, at the same time that Quince's Moonshine departs in response to what he mistakes as a cue in Pyramus' lament. Horrified by the sight of the bloody mantle, Pyramus is seized by an attack of rhetoric that includes an injunction expressing cosmic despair, "Moon, take thy flight!" (V.i.294). Moonshine complies, and the rest of the action takes place in indeterminate illumination—perhaps, as Theseus helpfully suggests, by starlight.

But, as is often pointed out, the vagaries of Moonshine in the play of "Pyramus and Thisbe" are no greater than those of the moon in the play of *A Midsummer Night's Dream*. Seldom has Phoebe exercised her prerogative of changeability with more virtuosity, starting out as an old moon with four days to go before becoming new, but thereafter waxing and waning in short bursts in order to suit the convenience or inconvenience of the various characters. Indeed, it was a wise decision of Bottom and his associates not to trust the calendar indicating that the moon would be shining on the night of Theseus' nuptials and hence to write Moonshine into the play. They were only imitating Shakespeare, who could and did write moonlight in or out at will. The best in this kind don't even have shadows unless the playwright's imagination can provide them with moonlight in defiance of calendars.

In reading the story of Pyramus and Thisbe both in Ovid and in Chaucer one is reminded of the theme of the country parson's sermon: the need to walk the straight and narrow path between good and evil. In many of their works Ovid and Chaucer both seem to walk the straight and narrow path between the serious and the comic, and nowhere does Chaucer walk the path more adroitly than in some of the legends.[17] "The Legend of Thisbe" is one of the most adroitly told of these. Like Ovid, Chaucer respects and brings out the childlike charm of the story, but even while he is careful that nothing overt should outrage the sentimentally inclined reader who is fond of the story, he somehow manages to leave it more open to the possibility of ridicule than Ovid had. Such low seriousness as the story has in Ovid is imparted by the metamorphosis of the mulberries by Pyramus' blood. This etiological purpose allows the story to be read backward, as it were, from the metamorphosis, and this provides a kind of justification for the absurd behavior of Pyramus, Thisbe, and the lioness. Melodrama receives some sanction when it serves a ritualistic function, and its exaggeration seems less. In the same way, Ovid's gruesome simile of the blood from Pyramus' body spurting like water from a broken pipe is justified because the metamorphosis requires that the blood get from the prostrate Pyramus up into the leaves of the tree.

Of course Chaucer also tells the story from a structuring *donnée*, but one of less dignity than Ovid's sanctification (and sanguinization) of the mulberry tree. This is the proposition assigned to the narrator of *The Legend of Good Women* by Alceste that women are always faithful in love and men are generally unfaithful. Thus in Chaucer Pyramus must die, not in order to color the fruit of a tree—and the elimination of this necessity enables Chaucer to reduce the pressure in Ovid's image of a broken pipe—but mostly in order to give Thisbe a chance to prove herself as faithful a lover as he. Deprived of its etiological excuse, the story becomes one of human behavior and, unfortunately, uncommonly silly human behavior. The lovers' charming innocence threatens at any moment to become mere incompetence, so that Pyramus's suicide, based on patently insufficient evidence of Thisbe's death, seems less an act of passion than of idiocy. Chaucer quietly yet effectively enhances the absurdity by lamenting, primly and rather unfairly, that Thisbe should abandon her friends in trust of a man she did not know very well, and also by letting Pyramus suggest that his failure to arrive at the tomb before Thisbe was due to habitual tardiness (Ovid leaves his lateness unexplained). One feels that in obedience to Alceste's command, Chaucer would like to have made it appear that Thisbe was a more faithful lover than Pyramus but, with no support for this from the plot, had to conclude that Pyramus was a virtually unique example of a faithful masculine lover. He does his best for Thisbe by allowing her a longer lament than Ovid did, full of splendid posturing: she hopes God will give other lovers better luck than she and Pyramus have had, suggests that no gentle woman should be so bold as to involve herself in such an adventure (as her own, presumably), and concludes by qualifying herself as a leading female contestant in the intersexual true-love competition:

> But God forbid but a woman can
> Ben as true and louing as a man, [910–11]

says she, plunging Pyramus' sword into her heart. By this kind of embroidery Chaucer comes close to making Ovid's story "the most lamentable comedy, and most cruel death of Pyramus and Thisbe"—a very good piece of work, and a merry.

When Chaucer wrote *The Legend of Good Women* he had already treated the Pyramus and Thisbe story in a serious context in *Troilus and Criseyde*; and when Shakespeare wrote *A Midsummer Night's Dream* he either had alrady treated the story in the serious context of *Romeo and Juliet* or else was about to do so—the former seems the more likely.[18] And both authors show in these other works their awareness of the perils of using so egregiously melodramatic a situation seriously, and both make some effort to propitiate the gods of absurdity who preside over the theatrics of such suicidal lovers under any name or in any context.

Chaucer's source for *Troilus*, Boccaccio's *Filostrato*, contains the Pyramus and Thisbe incident that Chaucer seems to have accepted happily, even enthusiastically, in his retelling. The incident occurs in Book IV of Chaucer's poem, after the lovers have learned separately of the exchange that has been arranged of Criseyde for Antenor and both have gone into throes of despair at the prospect of their separation. Pandarus interviews each in turn and arranges a tryst for them that night. The pathos that Boccaccio employs in describing the lovers' reactions to the news Chaucer exploits to the full, even to overflowing. He begins by following his source closely, but then, especially in dealing with Criseyde, he starts to cross the invisible line that separates very fine writing from overwriting. He assigns Criseyde

rather more tears than Boccaccio had, and increasingly purple
tears at that. Her hair, whose gorgeous blondness had been assumed but never specified in the earlier part of the poem, now
crowns her grief in lines as unkempt as she:

> Hir ownded heer, that sonnishe was of hewe,
> She rent, and eke her fingers long & smal
> She wrong full ofte.   [736–38]

When Pandarus comes to visit her to arrange the meeting with
Troilus, he observes that

> Her mightie tresses of her sonnishe heares,
> Unbroiden, hangen all about her eares.   [816–17]

This breach of decorum—appearing in his presence with the
mighty tresses of her sunnish hairs hanging unbraided about her
ears—persuades Pandarus that she is about to prove a martyr to
love. The large effort the narrator has made for so demanding
an occasion is suggested by the fact that Criseyde alone of Chaucer's characters possesses elegantly *ounded*, "waved," hair; and
the brassy coinage *sunnish* occurs, fortunately, only here in all
his works. Its innate vulgarity appealed naturally to Lydgate,
who applied it, inevitably, to his Criseyde's hair. I suppose one
should not think of Quince's Pyramus thanking Moonshine for
his sunny beams, but absurdity is, one feels, just around the
corner from the sunnish-haired Criseyde's grief.

At the lovers' reunion, after a tearful but wordless embrace
that the narrator manages to take three stanzas to describe, Criseyde cries, "O Joue, I dye, and mercy the beseche. / Helpe,
Troilus!" (1149–50). She then falls into a deathlike trance. Over
Troilus' subsequent actions—his kissing her cold mouth, laying
her body out straight, arranging it as one does a corpse to be
placed on a bier—Chaucer lingers lovingly. Without adding
much to Boccaccio's action he manages to make a more leisurely
presentation of it—though it is characteristic that where the Italian poet says Troilo felt his mistress all over for signs of life, the
English says chastely that Troilus could find none. Finally, after
he has definitely satisfied himself that Criseyde is dead, Troilus
draws his sword and addresses a farewell speech to Jove, to Troy,
to Priam, to his brothers, and to Criseyde. This is in Chaucer

substantially what it is in Boccaccio, though Chaucer's Troilus adds a Thisbe-like statement that no lover will ever be able to say that Troilus did not dare to die for love. A translation of Boccaccio's version of the end of Troilo's speech is as follows: "'And thou for whom sorrow doth so grip me and who dost send the soul from the body, do thou receive me'—Cressida he meant."[19] Boccaccio's inelegant but helpful explanation is a recognition that Troilo's rhetoric may have momentarily succeeded in losing the reader. The Italian idiom for "to mean" that Boccaccio used is *volere dire*, literally, "to wish to say." That is, Troilo wished to say that it was Criseida who should receive him. Now it may be that Chaucer was ignorant of the idiom, though he surely must have known the French equivalent, *vouloir dire*, and I think it more likely that he chose to be ignorant of it. In any case, in Troilus' speech *Criseida* is converted from the direct object of *volea dire*—he wished to say Criseida—to a vocative with the verb *ricevi*, "receive," and *volea dire* is translated literally:

> "And thou Criseide, o swete hart dere,
> Receiue now my spirite," would he sey,
> With swerde at hart, al redy for to dey. [1209–11]

It is a small point, but a very Chaucerian one. The English phrase *would he say*, while technically it can mean "he wished to say," in this context can only be the imperfect tense of *say*, that is, the tense of repeated or continuing action. "Would he say" gives, unfortunately, a quick cool glimpse of Troilus in prolonged posturing, with sword at heart but continuing indefinitely to address a host of absent friends and relatives, as well as the recumbent Criseyde. One is inevitably reminded of Dorigen in *The Franklin's Tale*, proving to herself conclusively that historical precedents demand that she commit suicide—and going on proving it "for a day or two," until her husband comes back from a trip and offers a solution to her dilemma. Troilus is caught in a situation in which the rhetoric that proves the need for action succeeds in postponing the action whose need it is proving, a situation characteristic of melodrama and one that always teeters on the brink of absurdity.

In any case, Criseyde regains her senses before her lover's protracted resolution to kill himself is carried out, and her revival
converts potential tragedy to tragedy manqué at best, and to
comedy at worst. The anticlimax that occurs when the two lovers are left alive after all the talk of death does not, one must
admit, add to the dignity of the occasion. One feels perhaps a
bit let down that so much fine deathbed speech has gone for
naught, and it is almost embarrassing to have the heroine
awaken before the hero finally gets around to broaching his
boiling bloody breast. Chaucer has allowed the humor latent in
the situation to peep out from behind the mask of tragedy. And
he now allows Criseyde's common sense to take over the action.
Having seen Troilus' drawn sword, she duly fulfills the Thisbe-
role, at least by speaking in the form of a past contrary-to-fact
condition: that is, she says that *if* she had come to and found
Troilus dead, she would have slain herself with his sword. There
is no need to doubt her ability thus to carry out the finest traditions of high romance, yet her practicality does not let her linger
in the role. "But ho," she says,

> for we haue right inough of this,
> And let vs rise and straite to bedde go,
> And there let vs speken of our wo.
> For by that morter whiche that I se brenne,
> Knowe I ful well that day is nat ferre henne.   [1242-46]

In a way this anticlimactic scene is the climax of the poem,
and everything that follows is continuing anticlimax. It is surely
the melodramatic climax of the poem, for from then on the tone
is in general one of subdued restraint. Troilus and Criseyde
graduate, as it were, from their Pyramus and Thisbe roles, and
the narrator relates the equivocal commonsense attitude of Criseyde and the gloomy musings of Troilus, torn between his
hope that his great romance will be restored to him and his de-
spairing instinct that it will not. The poem would have been a
much more satisfactory tragedy if the lovers had died bloodily
in this scene, but it would not have been the great poem it is.
Nor could Chaucer have written it: his respect for his fallible
heroine and idealistic, unrealistic hero was too large to give

them such an easy way out. His handling of the scene in Book IV reflects a vision of humanity that sees the absurdity in situations in which people try desperately to force reality to be what it is not—sees it, and sympathizes with their effort, though with a smile lurking in the syntax.

No perception of absurdity is, of course, permitted in the deaths of Romeo and Juliet. If Shakespeare learned anything from Chaucer about melodrama, it was to curb its rhetoric so that it does not become posturing, as it had begun to do in Troilus' farewell lament. In Romeo's farewell, his emphasis is on Juliet's beauty even in what he takes to be death, and this lends a kind of attractiveness to death. Romeo does use some of the formalized rhetoric of self-pity, but not enough to make the onlooker impatient with him. And Juliet's final words are of splendid brevity, touched with an irony that seems almost to defeat death's separation of the lovers:

> Poison, I see, hath been his timeless end.
> O churl, drunk all, and left no friendly drop
> To help me after? I will kiss thy lips,
> Haply some poison yet doth hang on them,
> To make me die with a restorative.   [V.iii. 162–66][20]

Juliet's easy acceptance of the situation helps persuade the onlooker to accept it, and indeed Shakespeare has from the beginning made it easy to accept the melodramatic conclusion by making it seem inevitable. Though malignant surprise is the soul of melodrama, at no point in the melodramatic plot of *Romeo and Juliet* do the lovers really seem to believe—nor does the audience believe—that the outcome will be, or could be, different from what it is, so that when death comes it comes almost as a friend, as it seems to be to Juliet. The only moments these lovers share are snatched from the real world, and from their first meeting on there seems no probability that they can fit their love into the demands the world puts on them. The kind of ex post facto suspense that melodrama normally arouses—Oh, if only this had happened instead of that!—is almost altogether lacking, despite the large number of melodramatic events in the play that one would expect to produce such ex post facto suspense. One never really sees any hope for the happier alternative, and since it is hope that leads one to look for sensible alternatives and to reject others as absurd or senseless, hope's exclusion much diminishes the perception of absurdity.

Yet Shakespeare makes his sacrifice to the gods of absurdity by writing into the play one of the most ludicrous scenes in all his works. I refer to scene v of act IV, where the Nurse, the Capulets, and Paris discover that Juliet has, presumably, died.[21] Now of course we know that she has not died and is merely drugged, and so we may perhaps be forgiven for taking their grief a little less than seriously, as we may also have done with Troilus' if we were not persuaded that Criseyde was dead. But those concerned think Juliet dead, so that their grief is genuine and should move us. Instead, however, Shakespeare gives us a scene exhibiting extravagant grief at its most outrageous. The mourners seem engaged in a contest of finding the right word for the situation, with the result that they sound as if they were in dire need of a thesaurus. The Nurse is hard put to find the mot juste for the day of Juliet's death, and Lady Capulet assists her in her frustrating search:

> *Nurse.* O lamentable day!   [17]
>   Look, look! O heavy day!   [18]
>   She's dead, deceas'd, she's dead, alack the day!
> *Lady Capulet.* Alack the day, she's dead, she's dead, she's
>   dead!   [23–24]
> *Nurse.* O lamentable day!
> *Lady Capulet.*   O woeful time!   [30]
>   Accurs'd, unhappy, wretched, hateful day!
>   Most miserable hour that e'er time saw . . . !   [43–44]
> *Nurse.* O woe! O woeful, woeful, woeful day!
>   Most lamentable day, most woeful day
>   That ever, ever, I did yet behold!
>   O day, O day, O day, O hateful day!
>   Never was seen so black a day as this.
>   O woeful day, O woeful day!   [49–54]

We are not very far away from Bottom-Pyramus' premature lament:

> O grim-look'd night! O night with hue so black!

> O night, which ever art when day is not!
> O night, O night, alack, alack, alack!   [V.i.168–70]

Paris fails to elevate the tone by embroidering on Nurse's elegant variation of *deceas'd* for *dead*:

> Beguil'd, divorced, wronged, spited, slain!
> Most detestable Death, by thee beguil'd,
> By cruel, cruel thee quite overthrown!
> O love, O life! not life, but love in death! [*correctio*]   [55–58]

And Old Capulet continues the search for suitable words to describe death's operation:

> Despis'd, distressed, hated, martyr'd, kill'd!
> Uncomfortable time, why cam'st thou now
> To murther, murther our solemnity?   [59–61]

Friar Lawrence's interruption, "Peace ho, for shame!" is a much-needed dash of cold water on this group of sorrowers trying out their vocabularies; but it occurs perhaps too late to prevent us from thinking of Pyramus' collection of alliterative synonyms for how the Fates may cause his death:

> O Fates, come, come!
> Cut thread and thrum:
> Quail, crush, conclude, and quell!   [V.i.274–76]

Variety is the spice of death.

Frank Kermode remarks that the scene in *Romeo* is one of the "more daring rhetorical adventures in all the tragedies," and that it contrasts the "reality of the love relationship" with the "relative falsity even of the grief of parents and Nurse and official lover." [22] It surely does enhance the simplicity of the lovers' language in grief, but I'm not sure it's fair to use the phrase "relative falsity" for the grief it describes. It seems to me that the grief is entirely sincere: it is merely absurd in its rhetorical overreaching and underachieving, and I think in a very subtle way it drains off the residue of absurdity from the main plot. It is something of a sleight-of-hand trick. It encourages one to recognize and face human absurdity, but channels the recognition onto recipients who will not be much harmed by it. Romeo and

Juliet are thus enabled to remain free and apart from the absurdity that is inherent in their story.

Troilus and Criseyde and Romeo and Juliet are in danger, as
Chaucer and Shakespeare were well aware, of becoming the
quick bright things who come to the confusion of Pyramus and
Thisbe in Peter Quince's play; or, worse, they're in danger of
being immortalized in a romance written by the narrator of *Sir
Thopas*. The best in this kind are but shadows. And though Theseus tells the artisans, "No epilogue, I pray you, for your play
needs no excuse. Never excuse" (V.i.341–42), nevertheless
Shakespeare himself resorts to an epilogue in which he reverts
to the insubstantiality of art that Chaucer and he had probed so
charmingly. Puck, alone on the stage, begins his lyrical farewell
with "Now the hungry lion roars" (V.i.357), reminding us that
lions are properties as useful to the best in this kind as to the
worst; and after Oberon and Titania have come and gone, Puck
ends the play with the forbidden epilogue. This begins with a
reference to Prologue's strangely punctuated apology at the beginning of the play of "Pyramus and Thisbe":

> If we offend, it is with our good will.
> That you should think, we come not to offend,
> But with good will.   [V.i.108–10]

This Puck restates to include the play of *A Midsummer Night's
Dream*:

> If we shadows have offended
> Think but this, and all is mended,
> That you have but slumber'd here
> While these visions did appear.
> And this weak and idle theme,
> No more yielding but a dream,
> Gentles, do not reprehend.   [V.i.409–15]

And the best in this kind recedes into the shadows.

2

The Lunacy of Lovers: *The Knight's Tale*, *The Merchant's Tale*, and *A Midsummer Night's Dream*

hakespeare's use in *A Midsummer Night's Dream* of two *Canterbury Tales* in addition to *Sir Thopas* is generally acknowledged, and in the new Arden edition Harold Brooks makes a scrupulous accounting of the many details that reflect Shakespeare's familiarity with the *Knight's* and *Merchant's Tales.*[1] My interest in this chapter is in relationships more subtle and less tangible than those that are generally discussed, involving themes and motifs that occur in the works of both authors and have a recognizable relationship despite differences in approach and in emphasis. I am once again following in the footsteps of Dorothy Bethurum, who was the first to point out Chaucerian influences on *A Midsummer Night's Dream* that go beyond catalogable instances of simple resemblance.[2] In general I find that the principal theme the two poets share, the irresponsibility of romantic love, leads them to speculate on and illustrate love's obsessiveness and its randomness: how quickly lovers surrender themselves to it, and how completely, unable to regard as worthy of consideration any matter not connected with their love; yet how haphazard the process of love is, with A falling head over heels in love with B so that B is all his mind can contemplate—until, that is, C comes along to replace B in A's mind and heart like one lantern slide replacing another. Also, in these works the lovers are assisted or hindered in their affairs—or simply tampered with—by supernatural powers who are as irresponsible as the mortals they interfere with, of whom, indeed, they are only distorted images. Love's responsibility thus takes on in both writers cosmic as well as comic dimensions.

Shakespeare's play is a cheerful one, with an outlook at least guardedly optimistic, though it surely offers no generalization to the effect that romantic love will always produce tidy pairs who will go on living happily ever after. The interpretation that is suggested when it is read in conjunction with the Chaucerian poems, however, is one that gives rather more weight than is usual to the darker side of romantic love, to the potential perils caused by the lovers' irresponsibility. The Chaucerian antecedents do not, to be sure, offer any justification for reading the play with Jan Kott as an exercise in erotic brutality,[3] but they do encourage one to heed the underlying emotional untidiness. This quality seems to me to make the play something less than an appropriate adjunct to a wedding, as Shakespeare is often said to have written it to be.[4] But perhaps the spirits of the celebrants at an Elizabethan marriage were so high as to be able to soar above the play's skeptical—even cynical—overtones, as have, indeed, the spirits of countless critics charmed by the delicate side of Shakespeare's fairyland. Still, I note with interest that the critic who wrote most eloquently about *A Midsummer Night's Dream* as "festive comedy" complained that its skeptical side had been badly neglected.[5] This side is, I believe, in part a legacy from Chaucer.

In discussing how Chaucer and Shakespeare treated the darker side of romantic love I do not want to suggest that either poet disapproved of romantic love or had moral reservations about it. Indeed, both poets treated the subject with little regard for morals. I find no moral in Chaucer's *Knight's Tale* unless it is that we should expect the worst: *The Merchant's Tale* has a more obvious moral, but as it concerns senile lechery, it is not one that is appropriate here. And I agree with Dr. Johnson that (in this play, at least) Shakespeare wrote "without any moral purpose"[6]—though I do not agree that his failure to do so constitutes a flaw. Art's educational function, pointing out the way

things are, is as valid as any moral one. And though romantic
love must be recognized as irresponsible, it is also a lot of fun
when it turns out well in fiction or in life, as it often does; and
it is a very interesting and moving sadness when it comes out
wrong, as it often does. The latter gives us *Romeo and Juliet*; the
former *A Midsummer Night's Dream*, which, as Bethurum says,
Shakespeare seems to have written "at a time when he was for
the moment unable to take love seriously."[7]

The most fully responsible character in Chaucer's *Knight's
Tale* and in *A Midsummer Night's Dream* is Theseus, Duke of Athens. But while this mentor-figure is often said to be the only
character that Shakespeare adopted from Chaucer without
change,[8] the second Theseus seems to me somewhat less mature, less philosophical, and a good deal more skeptical than the
first. Both Theseuses are, it is true, experienced, orderly, tolerant men who show becoming sympathy for the idiotic behavior
of a parcel of young lovers in the woods, whether the woods are
of fourteenth-century Athens-on-Thames or sixteenth-century
Athens-on-Avon. But the second Theseus draws as much from
Chaucer's Knight as he does from the Knight's Theseus, especially in his reluctance to speculate about matters beyond his
ken. Chaucer's Knight, after giving a remorselessly harrowing
account of Arcite's death, informs us, with a lightness of spirit
that some find shocking, that Arcite's spirit went somewhere,
but where he knows not, not having been there himself and
being no theologian. The Knight's Theseus, on the other hand,
has more assurance in such matters, and in his final speech in
the poem speaks of mourning for Arcite's death as folly, because
Arcite has escaped from "the foul prison of this life" (A 3058–
66). He does not, of course, pinpoint Arcite's final destination,
but it seems to be a better place than here, for his speech is an
attempt to establish the existence of a divine plan behind the
randomness that has controlled the events of *The Knight's Tale*.
But Shakespeare's Theseus shares the Knight's skepticism about
what he has not seen with his own eyes. Hippolyta's remark
about the lovers' confused story of their enchanted night in the
woods, "'Tis strange, my Theseus, that these lovers speak of,"
evokes from him the unillusioned reply,

> More strange than true. I never may believe
> These antique fables, nor these fairy toys. [V.i.2–3]

After thus denying the reality of a number of the fellow members of his cast, he continues with his famous speech on the lunatic, the lover, and the poet, who are of imagination all compact—a marvelous passage of imagination all compact that denies that creatures of the imagination can take on corporality. It is a delightful irony, and perhaps one a bit damaging to his dignity, that the skeptical Theseus begins his last speech in the play by mentioning the fairies in whom he disbelieves—

> The iron tongue of midnight hath told twelve.
> Lovers, to bed; 'tis almost fairy time— [V.i.349–50]

and upon ending it abandons the stage to the whole troop of presumably nonexistent fairies. Chaucer's Theseus argues for the existence of an unseen benevolent power; Shakespeare's Theseus argues against the existence of a power we can all see, whose benevolence exists for the exclusive benefit of Theseus, his bride, and, once they are married, their friends. Such blindness is surely related to love's blindness and the blindness of the other lovers in the play.

As political mentors, both Theseuses are admirable, enforcing the law as dukes of Athens should, while tempering justice with mercy in their handling of the lovers. Chaucer's Theseus heeds the request of Hippolyta and Emily to spare Palamon and Arcite when he comes upon them fighting in the woods for the right to love Emily; and he arranges the great tournament by which he hopes to settle the matter of which will have her. Shakespeare's Theseus invokes the law on Hermia at the request of her father Egeus, threatening her with death or else dedication to Diana if she persists in her refusal to marry Demetrius; but when after their night in the woods the lovers become unscrambled and Demetrius no longer wants to wed Hermia, Theseus bends the law and, despite Egeus' protests, allows her to marry Lysander. Both Theseuses mediate well between higher principles and lovers' needs.

Yet Shakespeare's Theseus is less loftily remote from the immediate problems of the play than Chaucer's. He is closer to the lovers' condition, for whereas Chaucer's Theseus and Hippolyta are already married when the poem's action begins, at the beginning of Shakespeare's play the couple has four days to wait before wedding. As a result, Chaucer's Theseus, though recently wed, seems, psychologically speaking, some distance beyond his bachelor days, but Shakespeare's Theseus seems to have a good deal of the bachelor about him, lamenting the time that must pass before he and Hippolyta are joined together. The common forebear of both dukes, the Theseus of Greek legend, had acquired in his bachelorhood an unenviable reputation as a philanderer and betrayer of women. Chaucer was perfectly well aware of this, and in *The Legend of Good Women* he celebrates with fine indignation Theseus' desertion of Ariadne in favor of her sister Phaedra. But in *The Knight's Tale* this aspect of Theseus' past is carefully suppressed, being merely glanced at in Theseus' own words when he contemplates the deplorable condition to which love has brought Palamon and Arcite:

> A man mote been a foole other yong or old.
> I wotte it by myself full yore agone,
> For in my tyme a seruaunt was I one
> And therefore . . . I knowe of loues pain.   [A 1812–15]

Whereas the amorous past of Chaucer's Theseus is thus neatly compressed into a statement suggesting merely some experience with love, and rendered relatively harmless by the word *servant* for "lover," Shakespeare's Theseus is assigned an erotic activity far more specific and genuinely damaging. In the course of their quarrel Oberon and Titania accuse one another of emotional involvement of an unspecified sort with Hippolyta and Theseus—an involvement that has, indeed, brought the King and the Queen of the Fairies by separate ways to Athens to honor the wedding of the mortals. Addressing Oberon, Titania refers to Hippolyta as "the bouncing Amazon, / Your buskin'd mistress and your warrior love," whereupon Oberon replies indignantly:

> How canst thou thus, for shame, Titania,
> Glance at my credit with Hippolyta,
> Knowing I know thy love to Theseus?
> Didst not thou lead him through the glimmering night

From Perigouna, whom he ravished;
And make him with fair Aegles break his faith,
With Ariadne and Antiopa?   [II.i.74–80]

This reference to four of Theseus' amorous exploits is something of an embarrassment to critics who are anxious to make
him not only a political mentor, but a moral one in the fashion
of his Chaucerian forebear. There is a tendency to sweep Theseus' womanizing under a moral rug.[9] Thus Harold Brooks
seems nervously defensive when he writes that Theseus'

> former delinquencies in love, at least his desertion of Ariadne,
> were notorious outside the play. Shakespeare treats them accord-
> ing to the precepts of panegyric: if a defect is too well known to
> be ignored, it must be brought in as favourably as possible. The-
> seus' amours are touched upon only once; if they did occur, it
> was perhaps under Titania's fairy influence; alternatively, they
> can be disbelieved, accepting his disavowal, as "the forgeries of
> jealousy."[10]

Still, Theseus' reputation was just as well known in Chaucer's
time, and he managed to ignore it, as did Shakespeare when he
handled Theseus the second time, in *The Two Noble Kinsmen*.
Although Shakespeare makes only a selection from North's catalog of Theseus' often violent erotic conquests (he omits Anaxo,
Peribea, Pherebaea, Joppa, and Helen "in her minoritie"), four
escapades, including one rape, is still a goodly number, well beyond the requirements of panegyric. Nor does it seem reasonable to try to shift the blame to Titania, making her role that of
the Marquise de Merteuil opposite Theseus' Valmont. Brooks
suggests that we ignore Oberon's assertions,[11] but that is to ignore Shakespeare's text. I must admit, however, that Shakespeare's text does not satisfy the question of what the exact nature of Theseus' relation to the Queen of the Fairies was, if he
did not believe in fairies in the first place. Perhaps all his earlier
amorous experiences had occurred in a dream.

In any case, the references to Theseus' escapades with women
modify one's impression of him as a mentor, and it is reasonable
to suppose that Shakespeare introduced them into the play in
order to add another dimension to its depiction of the effect on

human beings of sexual love. The references assimilate Theseus with the other masculine lovers of the play, both reducing him to their level and suggesting their potential elevation to his: as they mature, they may outgrow the idiocies in which they have been engaging, as, presumably, Theseus has done, renouncing his sportive past in the very serious act of wedding Hippolyta. She, incidentally, has also been given a touch of clay about the toes by Titania's accusation that Oberon had had her as his mistress. But gentlemanly Shakespeare does not further explore the matter of the ladies' past.[12]

Shakespeare's Theseus inherits from Chaucer the strife of lovers irrationally obsessed with their beloveds. In *The Knight's Tale*, the strife results from a triangle formed by two men in love with the same woman, and leads to the death of one of the men so that the other may have clear title to the lady. The heroes, Palamon and Arcite, are of equal merit as suitors, and are differentiated in ways that do not really affect the issue of which deserves her more. Either is equally suited or unsuited to a comic ending, marriage to Emily, or to a tragic ending, burial in a cold grave, alone without any company. To convert the plot from tragicomedy—or at least half-comedy, half-tragedy—to comedy, all Shakespeare had to do was to square the triangle, to add a second woman and arrange that one of the young men should finally fall in love with her.

This was an expedient that Shakespeare had used earlier in his career (again with Chaucer's *Knight's Tale* in mind)[13] in *The Two Gentlemen of Verona*. There he had squared the triangle his source in Montemayor had left him, the prototypes of Sylvia, Julia, and Proteus, by adding another man, Valentine, to take care of the extra woman in the triangle, whom Montemayor had killed off, as Chaucer did Arcite. Unhappily, however, Shakespeare had made the mistake of also adding a moral issue really irrelevant to the play by creating two lovers of highly dissimilar morality: Valentine, on the whole worthy if somewhat out of touch with reality, and Proteus, an archetypal cad who betrays both Julia and Valentine and threatens to rape Sylvia. Proteus' sudden reformation at the very last moment, while it persuades Valentine of its sincerity, does nothing to endear him to us, who are apt to feel that Julia, despite her passion for Proteus, might be better off dead than wed to him. The physical symmetry of the play's ending, with two couples joined in matrimony, is not matched by any inner conviction of symmetry.

In *A Midsummer Night's Dream* Shakespeare avoided involving himself again in odious comparisons by imitating in his two young lovers the similarity to one another of Chaucer's Palamon and Arcite—one might almost say their exchangeability. Shakespeare's Demetrius had loved Helena before the action of the play begins, but had transferred his affections to Hermia. He is thus potentially a fickle lover in contrast to Lysander, who has loved only Hermia. But the potential contrast goes nowhere, for once the play is under way it is hard to tell the lovers apart. Considered aside from their deplorable behavior in the woods, they both seem like nice enough young Athenian gentlemen of no distinguishing characteristics. They have both inherited from Chaucer's Palamon and Arcite an obsessive single-mindedness in love, though the object of their love may vary. Palamon and Arcite see Emily gathering flowers in the garden adjoining their dungeon tower in Athens, and each instantly invests all his emotional capital in loving her. Thereafter, both make their love for the distant, unmet Emily the food on which their egos feed. Palamon immediately claims exclusive rights to loving Emily on the grounds that he saw her first (A 1146), and goes on claiming such rights throughout the story, despite the fact that, as far as we can tell, he does not actually meet her for seven years and has hardly more than met her when he at last marries her. He is always ready—nay, anxious—to kill Arcite to protect his prior rights. Arcite, though he seems a touch cooler than Palamon, breaks his oath of sworn brotherhood to Palamon by insisting on going on loving Emily despite Palamon's claim to priority; and although, unlike Palamon, he perceives the absurdity of two prisoners fighting over a woman neither is ever likely to meet, he is willing, if necessary, to defend his right to love her to the death: he has no intention of imitating Valentine and handing over the emotional investment he has made in Emily to his friend, even though this seems to be what Palamon expects him to do. Bad behavior is their automatic response to love.

While Lysander and Demetrius love as intensely as Palamon and Arcite, the intensity of their hatred for one another is, if possible, even greater than that of their forebears. Comparatively speaking, Palamon and Arcite seem to wish to slay one another in the interests of a higher principle, as it were, and so without rancor. But Demetrius boasts that he is out to slaughter Lysander when he first follows his rival and Hermia into the woods, and once Lysander has received an application of Love-in-Idleness and wakes to erupt in love with Helena, his hatred for Demetrius explodes simultaneously. After announcing his love for Helena in three lines, he adds,

> Where is Demetrius? O how fit a word
> Is that vile name to perish on my sword!   [II.ii.105–06]

If we consider that at this time he presumably knows that Demetrius does not love Helena, then we must conclude that he hates him not as a rival but as one who has insulted his own new love by not loving her. But perhaps such a superabundance of hatred needs no reason. Subsequently, after Demetrius has received his application of essence-of-pansy and wakes to love Helena again, the two men become as occupied with killing one another as they are in making love to their bewildered mistress. They are prevented from mutual slaughter only by Hermia's physical intervention, and later by Puck's keeping them apart as they pursue each other through the woods.

But Shakespeare has added a new dimension as well as new intensity to the love-hate motif. The monomania of the lovers also expresses itself in the vehement loathing they both feel for the woman they just now loved passionately, as if an emotionally neutral state were impossible to them. When Helena follows Demetrius into the woods, his gentlemanly instincts yield instantly to revulsion. He begins patiently by telling her, "I love thee not, therefore pursue me not," but when that has no effect, he inquires sarcastically whether he is not telling her in plainest truth that he does not nor cannot love her. And when that does not dissuade her from following, he tells her

> Tempt not too much the hatred of my spirit;
> For I am sick when I do look on thee.   [II.i.211–12]

After Lysander wakes to love Helena and vows to kill Demetrius, he addresses the still sleeping Hermia thus:

> Hermia, sleep thou there,
> And never mayst thou come Lysander near!
> For, as a surfeit of the sweetest things
> The deepest loathing to the stomach brings;
> Or as the heresies that men do leave
> Are hated most of those they did deceive;
> So thou, my surfeit and my heresy,
> Of all be hated, but the most of me!   [II.ii.134–41]

After this blessing in reverse, he leaves her to face alone the uni-
versal hatred he has called down upon her. Titania, released by
Dian's bud from the effects of Love-in-Idleness, looks upon her
former beloved, the sleeping Bottom, and exclaims, "O how
mine eyes do loathe his visage now!" (IV.i.78) Lysander and Demetrius could not be more hateful to their former loves if both
the ladies had sprouted ass's heads.

While he added another character in order to square Chaucer's
triangle of love and hate, Shakespeare also departed from his
forebear by inventing two lively, noisy, articulate, self-willed,
and passionate women to replace the lovely, inert flower-maiden
of *The Knight's Tale*. It is true that Shakespeare's own flower-
maidens, such as Perdita, have a vitality Chaucer denied to Emily, but Hermia and Helena seem almost like cases of overcom-
pensation for Emily's general pallor. Their personalities are far
more distinct from one another than are their lovers'. Hermia,
short, dark, and fiery, is independent-minded and careful of her
chastity; Helena, tall, blond, and timid, is dependent and a bit
careless of her chastity. But the physical differences that help
individualize them do nothing to differentiate them as love-
objects. Their lovers can see Helen's beauty in a brow of Egypt
or vice versa, depending on which is the object of the young
men's passion at the moment. Indeed, while differentiating their
personalities, Shakespeare was at pains to emphasize the attractive nubility that makes them seem similar and susceptible to
interchange even when seen from a point of view more detached
than that of their momentary lovers. He went so far as to blur
the distinction he had made between them by assigning them

both trisyllabic names beginning with *H*, ending with *a*, and accented on the first syllable, so that either could, by simple substitution, grace a sonnet originally addressed to the other. Their equal attractiveness makes all the more absurd their lovers' change from ignoring one to loving her, or from loving her to hating her.

Both women are constant in love, and it is because of this that they are assigned by Shakespeare to carry out the motif, adapted from *The Knight's Tale*, of friendship destroyed by love.[14] Lysander and Demetrius have hardly enough strength of character to bear the burden of friendship. In Chaucer, the motif is a continuing but unemphasized presence: not only the friendship but the sworn bands of brotherhood are destroyed because of Palamon's and Arcite's love for Emily. Shakespeare's handling of this motif in *The Two Gentlemen of Verona* had resulted in the fiasco I mentioned earlier: Valentine's friendship for the horrid traitor Proteus is so strong that he refuses to let it be destroyed by their shared love for Sylvia; and when Proteus, in a speech of fewer than five lines, repents his wickedness, Valentine magnanimously exclaims, "All that was mine in Sylvia I give thee" (V.iv.84), thus presenting to him the understandably speechless Sylvia. In *A Midsummer Night's Dream* Shakespeare offers what may be a rueful echo of this piece of generosity: Lysander, now in love with Helena as a result of Puck's mistake, says to Demetrius (in a rare moment when he is not trying to kill him),

> here, with all good will, with all my heart,
> In Hermia's love I yield you up my part.   [III.ii.164–65]

But of course this offer reflects no friendship: in giving Hermia to Demetrius he is actually assigning him a fate he thinks worse than death.

Helena is the chief spokesman of the theme of broken friendship that Shakespeare's male lovers seem unworthy of sustaining. Her speech describing the friendship of her and Hermia when they were children is as touching as any in the play, exceeding in depth of feeling any expression of love between the sexes.[15] Unfortunately, though very comically, the delicacy of Helena's speech is marvelously counterpointed by the savagery of the two women's quarrel, and especially by that of Hermia, who makes up in ferocity what she lacks in size. "How low am I, thou painted maypole?" she asks Helena while threatening to reach up and scratch out her eyes. And Helena, who has spoken so lovingly of their happy childhood, has another sort of memory of little Hermia:

> She was a vixen when she went to school,
> And though she be but little, she is fierce.   [III.ii.324–25]

The theme of friendship remembered recurs more harmoniously when another woman in the play, Titania, says that the reason she has withheld the little Indian boy that Oberon so desires is her love for his mother, dead in childbirth, for whose sake she is bringing up the boy. Shakespeare's women take from Chaucer's men the responsibility of carrying on the theme of friendship

While I admire Hermia and Helena for their constancy, I must admit that I can't see what they see in Lysander and Demetrius. But neither in *The Knight's Tale* nor in *A Midsummer Night's Dream*—nor, perhaps, in a world less shadowy—is knowledge of the character of one's beloved a requisite for romantic love. Helena observes that "love looks not with the eyes, but with the mind" (I.ii.234), and the image in the mind is, psychologically if not physically, a perfectly satisfactory substitute for the reality, especially if the image is nurtured by occasional glimpses of an attractive reality. Palamon and Arcite see Emily gathering flowers, and the image is powerful enough in their minds so that they can go on loving her for years without necessarily even meeting her. Spenser might well have taken Chaucer's love triangle and squared it by adding a false Emily on the model of false Florimell, a fair image constantly on the move that either Palamon or Arcite could have been set off happily chasing for the rest of his life while the other settled down with the real Emily. It is the idea of the person that one loves, not necessarily the person.

Perhaps the chief difference in the love relationships of Chaucer's poem and Shakespeare's play is that in the former the beloved lady Emily loves neither one of her lovers and, indeed, does not know one of them exists until relatively late in the action, when the two knights are discovered fighting over her in the woods. Ironically, Emily is in a sense largely excluded from her own story's action. Nor would she have minded being permanently excluded from it. She is a contented young Amazon devoted to Diana, and she is able to develop no preference for either of the knights over the other. When she prays to Diana that she may remain her votary and a maid, she does express the wish that if she has to marry one of the young men she may marry him who loves her best (A 2323–25). This is the only recognition by any of the young people in either *The Knight's Tale* or *A Midsummer Night's Dream* (except, perhaps fleetingly by Hermia and Lysander at the beginning of the play) that love is a reciprocal business and that the beloved's emotional predisposition is all-important to the very existence of a love affair. Practical-minded despite her passivity, Emily approves of Arcite when he wins the tournament and feels dreadful when he dies; but after finally wedding Palamon she lives happily ever after with him. One feels, however, that she would have lived just as happily with Arcite, had he lived. It is unfair to cast doubt on the constancy of Hermia and Helena, but I am not certain the effect of the play would have been much different if Oberon and Puck between them had managed to drop the magic distillation in the eyes of both the women and of Lysander, and had them wake in such a way that Hermia loved Demetrius, and he her, and Helena Lysander, and he her. This solution, the opposite of the play's, would have pleased Egeus, who wanted Hermia to marry Demetrius, and would have made it unnecessary for Theseus to bend the Athenian law in Hermia's favor for her failure to do so. And it is hard to see what difference it would have made to the male lovers, who had loved both women in turn.

The cheerful cynicism about young love, especially its interchangeability, that infests *The Knight's Tale* and the play is increased by the supernatural machinery that interferes with the course of love, true or otherwise, in both works. In *The Knight's Tale*, the machinery consists of the planet-deities who eventually decide the issue of which young man gets Emily. When Theseus builds the lists in which the great tournament is to be fought by the knights and their respective forces for possession of Emily, he erects temples to each of the three deities of whom the three principals in the affair are votaries. Before the tournament, Palamon prays to Venus in her temple that he may win Emily, and the goddess signifies that he will; Arcite prays in Mars's temple that he may win the tournament, and Mars signifies that he will; in Diana's temple, Emily prays that she may remain unwed, and gets a negative but at least honest answer. Up in heaven a quarrel at once breaks out between Venus and Mars, because Venus has promised Palamon Emily and Mars has promised Arcite the victory by which he will presumably get Emily. In order to settle the quarrel between this pair of formerly adulterous immortals, old Saturn promises to devise a scheme by which everything will come out all right. His expedient is the simple brutal one of removing Arcite from contention by having him killed in an equestrian accident after winning the tournament. The solution has nothing to do with the merits of Palamon or Arcite, having been devised to ensure not justice on earth but peace in heaven. The planet-deities of *The Knight's Tale* have the pettiness but not the dignity of their Homeric ancestors: one feels that neither Venus nor Mars would have minded the least breaking a promise to a votary if it had not been that the other would become the beneficiary. These gods are as wayward as any mortals.

Although Shakespeare did not adopt this potentially tragic machinery, some of its spirit of arbitrariness, of randomness, spills over into his comedy. Moreover, the surplus of cynicism in Chaucer's *Merchant's Tale* has also bequeathed a portion to *A Midsummer Night's Dream*. Pluto and Proserpina, the prototypical participants in the kind of marriage *The Merchant's Tale* deals with, interfere in the marital affairs of an old man and his lovely young wife. As Tyrwhitt first suggested, Pluto and Proserpina provided Shakespeare with the models for Oberon and Titania. Chaucer demoted the ancient mythic couple to the status of quarrelsome English fairies, Pluto the King and Proserpina the Queen. This royal pair are enjoying the beauty of the garden that the blind old lecher January had built for love-making when they see his young wife, May, directing a young squire to ascend into a pear tree, where, with the unwitting aid of her husband, she intends to consummate her adulterous love with the squire. Pluto, seeing what May is up to, with splendid self-righteousness delivers to Proserpina a twenty-line homily on the wickedness of women—"your wickedness" he says to Proserpina, though the immediate exemplar is May. He vows to restore January's sight so that January will fully comprehend May's harlotry: Pluto shares medieval antifeminists' sense of obligation to make husbands aware of the wickedness, real or potential, of their wives. The former God of the Underworld seems wholly to have forgotten how he acquired Proserpina, though Chaucer has just reminded the reader of Pluto's rape of the lovely young girl in Etna. He is now behaving as if Proserpina had trapped him into a marriage he did not want. Proserpina, naturally offended by Pluto's antifeminist discourse, gives her word that she will provide May, and all women after, with a sufficient answer when caught in a compromising situation, and then proceeds to rebut Pluto's homily with a homily of her own almost twice as long. Thereafter, Pluto grudgingly calls for peace, but vows to keep his word to restore January's sight, as Proserpina vows to keep hers to give May a sufficient answer.[16]

In recasting this quarrelsome couple of immortals as Oberon and Titania, Shakespeare borrowed the genuine fairy name Oberon from Lord Berners' *Huon de Burdeux*, but went to Ovid for Titania, whom he had to demote just as Chaucer had had to demote Proserpina: Ovid's Titania referred either to Diana or to Circe. Oberon and Titania are a more actively unhappy married couple than their Chaucerian forebears, and are, unlike them, guilty of marital infidelity—at least they accuse each other of amorous dalliance: Titania with Theseus, and Oberon with Hippolyta as well as Phillida, whom he wooed disguised as Corin. Like Theseus, Oberon is sometimes said to be a mentor-figure, benevolently interfering in mortal affairs in order to straighten out lovers' entanglements. Thus Harold Brooks, following and summarizing a number of critics, seeks to extenuate Oberon's treatment of Titania by shifting the blame to her. According to Brooks, Oberon's punishment of Titania is designed to reunite her with him; on his own terms, certainly, but it is of course she who is principally at fault. Her attachment to her dead friend's child has become an obsession. It is perhaps (Puck may imply this) high time the boy was weaned from maternal dandling to be bred a knight and huntsman. However that may be, in preferring him above her husband Titania has got her priorities wrong; the worse when she has the responsibility of royal consort in the fairy world.[17]

Shame on you, Titania, for holding out on that nice male chauvinist King of the Fairies!

One can, I suppose, argue with a modicum of reason that Oberon is justified in punishing Titania for her willfulness—though to allow her to acquire a lover with an ass's head seems more fiendish than kingly. But it seems to me that the obsession is as much Oberon's as Titania's. I see small grounds for thinking that Oberon was concerned only with the child's education: his position seems to be closer to Ganymede's than to Richard Feverel's.[18] Nor is it clear that Titania deserted Oberon any more because of her love for the Indian boy than because of his love for the Indian boy, whom he wished to deprive her of and whom he seemed to prefer to her. If either Oberon or Titania is obsessive, both are, and together or alone they are very poor models for married couples. Despite Brooks's certainty—note that sinister "of course"—that Titania is in the wrong, I doubt that Shakespeare favored Oberon over Titania (it is Brooks who reduces her from "Queen" to "consort") any more than Chaucer did Pluto over Proserpina.

Even Oberon's interference in the love story is not free of the malice that he shows to Titania. Though he professes to be moved by pity for Helena when he instructs Puck to put the drops in Demetrius' eyes, his action remains a by-product of his spitefulness toward another woman, Titania. It was this that caused him to send for the drops in the first place. Like Pluto's pity for January in *The Merchant's Tale*, Oberon's pity for Helena is mixed with a malicious desire to get back at his wife, to take revenge for the jealousy she has caused him.[19] Moreover, it is not clear that he expects the administering of the drops to accomplish any really felicitous purpose. His order to Puck to put the fluid in the Athenian's eyes is accompanied by the strange prediction that before Helena leaves the woods, Demetrius will seek her love and she shall flee from him.[20] This seems an outcome more calculated to wreak vengeance on Demetrius than to do anything beneficial for Helena. Spitefulness twice infects Oberon's presumed benevolence. He does, of course, try to rectify Puck's mistake and later has him prevent Lysander and Demetrius from killing each other. But an immortal who straightens out a mess he has himself caused hardly acquires thereby the stature of a benevolent mentor.

Oberon commands powerful magic, but his use of it, as far as mortals are concerned, is inefficient: a magician more careful might have given Puck clearer instructions on how he should recognize Demetrius. When Prospero, for example, tampers with meteorology, he is more careful to limit the effects of the storm he brews up to those in whom he has a direct interest.[21] But Oberon's and Titania's quarrel has caused ruinous weather for farmers and for everyone else—widespread flooding, horrid rheumatic mists, and confusion of the seasons are the by-products of immortal sulks. Just so had Pluto's far-off rape of Proserpina caused as its side effect the introduction of the seasons and of winter to mankind. These sets of immortals seem hardly to qualify as benevolent dei ex machina.

Oberon's charming assistant,[22] Puck, is without benevolence for mortals. When he learns that he has anointed the wrong man's eyes he is delighted, for he considers the resulting confusion excellent sport. Jan Kott reminds us, a bit too portentously,[23] that the name Puck is derived from an old word for devil; in Langland the Pouke is sometimes the Devil. Fortunately, Puck's mischief-making repertory is limited to petty tricks, but his etymological ancestry does suggest that the master he serves, apparently voluntarily, is, as Kott and others have suggested, not one of those nice nineteenth-century fairies who go around being kind to selected children. Oberon seems to me closer to the Fairy King of the English romance *Sir Orfeo*, who kidnaps ladies sleeping under grafted trees and treats all but a few members of the human race with cruelty—who has, indeed, something of the Devil about him, who is devoid of altruism. One ought also to note the strict limitation of the one un-questioned instance of the altruism of Oberon and Titania:[24] in blessing (if that is the right word) the marriage of Theseus and Hippolyta they are doing a very special favor to a couple that has shared their own promiscuity. It is delightful that immortals should be so thoughtful in regard to their mortal former loves, but the delight is not untinged with cynicism.

From *The Merchant's Tale* there comes to the play the shadow of another cynical proposition—an implicit question whether the interference of the supernatural beings in mortal affairs is not, at times, redundant: in the tale, the question is whether January and May are given something they could not use or already had. Long before old January loses his eyesight the Mer-chant has begun to ring the changes on the theme of love's blindness. Of January's choosing May "of his owne aucthoritee" the Merchant observes that "love is blinde al daie and maie not see" (E 1598)—a platitude so tautologically expressed as to be almost shocking. When January goes blind physically, his out-rageous jealousy for May draws the following comment from the narrator:

> O January, what might the it auaile
> Tho thou mightest se as fer as shippes saile;
> For as good is a blinde man disceiued be,
> As to be disceiued when that a man may se. [E 2107–10]

When, through Pluto's magic, January sees his wife copulating with her lover, she explains to him that she has tried to cure his blindness by "struggling" with a man up in a tree, and he is quickly persuaded that he has not seen what he has seen. The gift of restored sight instead of curing his real blindness merely reinforces it: before he did not see what he could not see; now he cannot see what he does see. The gift that May receives from Proserpina may be equally redundant. In one of the analogues of the Pear Tree Story the roles of Pluto and Proserpina are played by Christ and St. Peter. The Apostle sees a blind man about to be cuckolded by his wife up in a tree and asks the Lord to restore the man's sight so that he can see his wife's shame. Christ does this, but not before remarking that it will make no difference—the woman will persuade her husband he has seen nothing. The wife uses the same answer as May does, and her husband thanks her for curing his blindness.[25] Neither she nor May needs supernatural assistance.

Something of this cynicism underlies the surface of the action of *A Midsummer Night's Dream* when Oberon tampers with the eyesights of Lysander and Demetrius. Demetrius had loved Helena previously; but since it needed no application of Love-in-Idleness to make him abandon Helena and love Hermia, one may properly wonder whether he is not perfectly capable of abandoning Hermia and reverting to Helena without supernatural assistance. And it is possible to take the faithful Lysander's abandonment of Hermia and pursuit of Helena because of Puck's mistake as an image of what might happen without Puck's interference. The magic drops made him love Helena, but the fact that his undying love for Hermia turns into abusive hatred seems to have been his own fault, suggesting that love's enchantment, whether literal or figurative, causes complete loss of control as well as of discrimination. One might say with Puck, coarsely, that all Jack really needs is a Jill, a man needs only a mare, and it hardly matters which one. One recalls with horror the treacherous lover Proteus' rationalization, after his sudden reform in *The Two Gentlemen of Verona*, of his quick transfer of affection from Sylvia to Julia:

> What is in Sylvia's face, but I may spy
> More fresh in Julia's with a constant eye?　　　[V.iv.114–15]

Never was constancy more inappropriately invoked; but the infelicitous rhetoric does emphasize the remarkable exchangeability of young love. Shakespeare's name for the love-causing eye-drop is less than respectful. He might well have called it after the pansy, from which it is distilled, and which offers the possibility of many a pretty poetic play; or he might have given it some splendidly pharmaceutical name like Lyly's *anacamphoritis*, which had the same effect on those to whom it was administered. But Love-in-Idleness suggests something ephemeral, an irresponsible drug whose effects are short-lived and of little consequence.

But Oberon suggests that Lysander, Demetrius, Hermia, and Helena will remain faithful lovers forever, whether or not they are still under the influence of the magic drops, and there is no reason to doubt his word. Lasting marriages do emerge from the shambles of romantic love, whether as a result of Love-in-Idleness or of an enchantment less recondite. The play celebrates both the beauty and the foolishness of romantic love, as well as the fragility, the precariousness, the hit-or-miss chanciness of its universe, which includes gods, fairies, and mortals. The cynicism, which is sharpened by an awareness of the Chaucerian sources, does not in any way impair the cheerfulness of the story of confused young lovers in which, thanks in part to a bit of inadvertent aid from the Other World, everything comes out right in the end. It does not impair the cheerfulness, but enriches it by undermining it, by questioning the easiness of happy endings and suggesting their rareness: there, but for sheer luck, go Pyramus and Thisbe.[26]

In *A Midsummer Night's Dream* occurs what I suppose to be Shakespeare's most frequently quoted line, Puck's exclamation at the behavior of the lovers, "Lord, what fools these mortals be!" (III.ii.115) But, as Dorothy Bethurum long ago pointed out,[27] it is Chaucer who had earlier written a line that better summarizes *A Midsummer Night's Dream*. Chaucer's Theseus, observing how dreadfully Palamon and Arcite have wounded one another in fighting for a woman who hardly knows they are alive, exclaims at the horrendous power of love: "Who maie be a foole, but if he loue?" (A 1799). The two poets agree that lovers are lunatics living in a dream world; but both would probably also agree that the dream world must underlie the real world as the real world underlies that of the dream.

3

Love, War, and the Cost of Winning:
The Knight's Tale and *The Two Noble Kinsmen*

t is the chief misfortune of one who is considering the relation of Chaucer to Shakespeare that there is no way to avoid that most distressing of plays, *The Two Noble Kinsmen*. Though the play was written in collaboration with Fletcher, it still represents Shakespeare's most direct and unquestionable use of a Chaucerian source—as the Prologue to the play proclaims it to be—and it would be dereliction of duty for me to ignore it. It's not that it is a bad play (though I don't think it a very good one), but that it is a very unpleasant one in which the dark side that Shakespeare saw in *The Knight's Tale* when he was writing *A Midsummer Night's Dream* is fulsomely re-expressed. But rereading the play along with its source may enhance one's appreciation of it, as Philip Edwards' brilliant article "On the Design of *The Two Noble Kinsmen*" has demonstrated.[1] I am both fortunate to have this article as a model of what good criticism can do for the play and unfortunate that it has anticipated my study of the Chaucerian connections. I am grateful also for Ann Thompson's discussion of the play's use of the Chaucerian original,[2] and to Clifford Leech's remarks in his introduction and note on the source in the Signet edition of the play.[3] Perhaps no play of Shakespeare's has inspired a smaller body of criticism or one of higher quality. Uncertainty about which portions are Shakespeare's and which Fletcher's has probably put many critics off. In my own study I accept as Shakespeare's those portions that Leech says are accepted by the majority of Shakespeareans,[4] and I confine my discussion mostly to these; I give notice when I find it necessary to talk about something of Fletcher's.

Chaucer's *Knight's Tale* is often spoken of—rightly, I think—as a philosophical romance. That is, it has the plot and characters proper to a romance (though it lacks a villain), but the author's interest lies less in them than in the attitudes toward human life that they offer. The heroes of the story are no more than moderately interesting people. Their story concerns the struggle between them to assert their right first to love, and later to possess, Emily, sister-in-law of Duke Theseus of Athens, from whose prison Palamon and Arcite first see their beloved. On seeing her, they begin a quarrel that ends only after they have fought in a great tournament arranged by Theseus to determine the issue of which should have Emily, a tournament that Arcite wins only to be fatally injured in an equestrian accident while riding around the lists in triumph. Some years after his death, Theseus economically weds Emily to Palamon, a happy event that Theseus uses as an excuse for a fine speech in which he argues for the existence of a divine plan operating behind the randomness of such events as the death of the triumphant Arcite. Palamon and Emily are described as living happily ever after.

The issue that seems to interest Chaucer in *The Knight's Tale* is the dominant role of chance in determining the course of human life.[5] Although Palamon and Arcite have some individuality, it is not large—though I must confess that I find more distinction between them than I once did, as a result of comparing them to their descendants in the play. But even in Chaucer there is, as I have said, no moral difference between the two. They are both exponents of the highest kind of chivalric idealism. The Knight observes the destruction of their friendship by their amorous rivalry, but accepts it, as does the tolerant Theseus of *The Knight's Tale*, as an unsurprising operation of love's folly, something to regret, but also to accept. While love is obviously not the same as chance, the good-humored Knight almost makes it seem so, because like chance it buffets the young men so mercilessly. But it is pure chance that makes them prisoners to Theseus and lovers of Emily; it is chance that Theseus' friend

Pirithous, who had known Arcite previously, visits Theseus and, learning that Arcite is his prisoner, obtains Arcite's freedom. Chance brings it about that when Palamon finally escapes from prison, he hides outside Athens in the same part of the woods to which Arcite comes early in the morning to celebrate May, so that Palamon overhears Arcite talking to himself about his love for Emily, whom he serves under a disguise. It is chance that guides Theseus' hunt the next day to the spot where Arcite and Palamon are fighting to the death over the right to love Emily. And finally, it is chance from the human point of view—it is actually the operation of a planet-deity—that causes Arcite's death, upsetting Theseus' carefully ordered attempt to settle the issue of which should have Emily in a correctly chivalric way. Against this background, Theseus' final suggestion that all is for the best has something of a hollow ring; nor does he argue that Arcite was in any way less deserving of Emily than Palamon. Indeed, it is possible to read Theseus' speech not as a philosophical consideration of the role of chance in human events but rather as a statement of man's need, in a world so hostile, to *believe* that a divine plan exists; to believe otherwise is to give in to despair.

Aside from describing the misadventures of the two heroes, a surprisingly large part of the narrative is given over to symbolic description that reinforces the idea of a world of little felicity. I have mentioned the temples that Theseus built to the three deities of whom Palamon, Arcite, and Emily are votaries, but I have not dwelt on how depressing these temples of Venus, Mars, and Diana are. In Venus' temple (A 1914–66) there is a statue of the naked goddess but, aside from that bit of allurement, the decorations portray her effect on humanity largely in terms of the pain, folly, corruption, and degradation that she causes.[6] Mars's temple (A 1967–2050) is filled with images of horrid death by steel and fire—war, murder, suicide, and accidents as awful as the sow devouring the child lying in its cradle. Diana (A 2051–88) too is associated with the pain she has caused: her fierce vengeance on Actaeon, Callisto, and that king whose neglect of sacrifice brought on his land the Calydonian boar. In addition to these disagreeable depictions of how the gods show their power over humanity—which, let me repeat, the Knight takes in stride—there is an unedifying glimpse of their behavior in heaven: Venus and Mars quarreling when they learn of the conflicting promises they have made to their votaries, so that both Palamon and Arcite seem to have been promised Emily. It is said that the gods quarrel so persistently that Jupiter is hard put to keep order in heaven, and only the most baleful of the planet-deities, Saturn, can offer a solution to the dilemma (A 2438–52). Before he does so, Saturn goes out of his way to explain his operation in the world of mortals, a description even more depressing than the wall paintings in the temples (A 2453–69): he boasts that he is responsible for drowning, imprisonment, strangling, hanging, poisoning, rebellion, earthquakes, conspiracy, and pestilence, a catalog he concludes by telling Venus to cheer up, for he will find a way to allow both her and Mars to redeem their promises. The device he uses, of course, is Arcite's fatal horseback accident.

This heavy strain of pessimism underlying *The Knight's Tale* apparently appealed to a Shakespeare who, nearing the end of his active career, was in a mood far different from that which produced *A Midsummer Night's Dream*, although *The Knight's Tale*'s pessimism had not entirely escaped him then. But no play in the canon contains more horrid images than *The Two Noble Kinsmen*—Shakespeare might be said to have plundered the paintings on the temple walls of *The Knight's Tale*. Yet whereas the horrors in Chaucer seem mostly charged to the gods above, Shakespeare puts them back where they started, in the hearts of people. It is something of an anomaly that in *The Knight's Tale*, despite Palamon and Arcite's disastrous quarrel over love, the human beings seem to behave somewhat better than the immortals do, and are at least partially independent of them. Palamon and Arcite are both obviously followers of Venus in loving Emily, yet one feels that she has less impact on their characters than on their eventual fate. The gods, that is, seem to control fatal machinery rather than human action. Thus they have an objective existence that they lack in Shakespeare. The characters in the play do speak of the gods as having objective existence, but they are not permitted to appear on stage—except for Hymen, god of marriage, who has a nonspeaking ritualistic role in the first scene. But Venus and Mars and Diana are not seen as manipulating mankind from above, but from within, with the result that the play's characters themselves seem to have come down from the Knight's temple walls. Yet it is true that this awareness is denied the play's characters, and they pretend, like the characters in *The Knight's Tale*, to be moved by irresistible impulses dictated from above, though with far less reason.

As several critics, most compellingly Edwards, have pointed out, Venus is the most powerful malignant influence in the play; but in actual fact she shares her malignancy with Mars, from whose handiwork Shakespeare takes many of the play's most gruesome images. Theseus, a mighty warrior who has acquired his bride-to-be, Hippolyta, by defeating her in battle, is a votary of Mars; and Hippolyta also is a votary of Mars, having once been a mighty warrior herself and Queen of the Amazons—a fact that Chaucer passes over with the merest of mentions (A 822). As an Amazon, her sister Emilia should also be a votary of Mars, but Shakespeare here follows Chaucer's lead and pictures her almost entirely as a votary of Diana, who was, of course, an Amazon's second tutelary deity. Shakespeare's Palamon and Arcite, as both gallant˜and chivalrous young knights, are Martian by profession and temperament, and while they come under the sway of Venus, the only way they can express the love in their hearts is by fighting one another to the death. For this combination of the Martian and the Venerean (the arbitrary assignment of one knight to Venus and the other to Mars in both Shakespeare and Chaucer is a matter to which I shall return), the union of Theseus and Hippolyta provides an appropriate if inexact image: love results from conquest, or conquest is necessary in order to open a path for love.

Mars is the supplier of the most horrid images. The Elizabethan *sententia*, that war is the great purgative, receives perhaps over-eloquent expression in Arcite's prayer to Mars:

> O great corrector of enormous times,
> Shaker of o'er-rank states, thou grand decider
> Of dusty and old titles, that heal'st with blood

The earth when it is sick, and cur'st the world
O' th' plurisy of people!   [V.i.62–66][7]

But if this is only conventional horridness, the speech of a victim of Mars, the widow of King Capaneus, one of the queens who asks Theseus for help in the play's first scene, might make even an Elizabethan wince: Creon, she says, will not allow them to burn their dead husbands' bodies,

> nor to take th'offense
> Of mortal loathsomeness from the blest eye
> Of holy Phoebus, but infects the winds
> With stench of our slain lords. O pity, Duke,
> Thou purger of the earth.   [I.i.44–48]

Theseus' duty is, like Mars's, to purge the earth. Another of Mars's victims, the Second Queen among the widows, asks Hippolyta to kneel to Theseus and pray him to help:

> Lend us a knee;
> But touch the ground for us no longer time
> Than a dove's motion when the head's pluck'd off.   [I.i.96–98]

I don't know whether the special providence that governs the decapitation of a dove belongs to Mars or Saturn; probably Mars, for the Queen continues her plea that Hippolyta should importune Theseus to take martial vengeance:

> Tell him if he i' th'blood-siz'd field lay swoll'n,
> Showing the sun his teeth, grinning at the moon,
> What you would do.   [I.i.99–101]

But nothing in this business of "rotten kings or blubber'd queens" quite matches Hippolyta's imagery when she and Emilia are bidding farewell to Pirithous, off to join his friend Theseus' campaign against Creon:

> We have been soldiers, and we cannot weep
> When our friends don their helms, or put to sea,
> Or tell of babes broach'd on the lance, or women
> That have sod their infants in (and after eat them)
> The brine they wept at killing 'em.   [I.iii.18–22]

This reminiscence of maternal cannibalism, outdoing anything of Lady Macbeth's at her bloodiest, though emanating from that symbol of womanly meekness, a bride-to-be, illustrates all too clearly the almost gratuitous preoccupation with horrors that Shakespeare adopts from the starker side of his Chaucerian source. Whereas Venus may be the most malignant influence in the play, the world in which she works is wholly Mars's.

As I said earlier, I find more distinction in Chaucer between the characters of the two chief victims of Venus and Mars, Palamon and Arcite, as a result of reading the play than I had noticed before. That is because such differences as Chaucer wrote in or inherited from Boccaccio, the dramatists wrote out. They did this largely, I suppose, to prevent our taking sides in the quarrel and thus being distracted from the more important issue of the sad destruction of their friendship: Shakespeare may have remembered the disastrous effect that his differentiation of Valentine and Proteus had on the issue of friendship in *The Two Gentlemen of Verona*. The result of the changes in the play is badly to disappoint those who admire Shakespeare for his character portrayals. In Chaucer, Palamon is the more impetuous, the more excitable, of the two knights, jumping at decisions and translating his ideas into action as soon as they come to him. When he first sees Emily from his prison he decides at once that she is a goddess—Venus, actually—and he falls on his knees to pray her to release Arcite and him from their imprisonment (A 1101–11). When Arcite sees her a moment later and vows his undying love for her, Palamon becomes furious and rightly, if somewhat prematurely, accuses him of violating his oath of sworn brotherhood by "hindering" Palamon's love. Throughout the tale, Palamon continues to insist that Arcite's loving Emily is an injury to him, Palamon, and when, years later, he overhears Arcite in the woods speaking of his love for Emily, he insists that they fight to the death to decide who shall love—not, mind you, who shall have, but who shall love—Emily. When Theseus discovers them fighting, it is Palamon who informs him who they are—his enemies—and asks him to put them both to death (A 1715–41). Poor Arcite never gets a word in edgewise in the whole scene.

Palamon appears in Shakespeare and in Fletcher, who is responsible for many of his scenes, pretty much as he does in Chaucer, where he already illustrates that chaotic influence of Mars and Venus which the play is exploring. Arcite, however, suffers a good deal of change. In Chaucer, he is the steadier, more thoughtful, and more sensible of the two, and he even has a touch of humor. When Palamon claims exclusive rights to loving Emily upon first sight of her, Arcite perceives the absurdity of their fighting over a woman neither is ever likely to attain:

> We striuen as did the hounds for the bone
> That fought all day & yet her part was none.
> Ther cam a cur while that they wer so wroth
> And bare away the bone from hem both   [A 1177–80]

It is true that when Palamon bases his right to loving Emily on his having seen her first, Arcite responds with a quibble of his own: he points out that Palamon thought she was a goddess, and claims that his own recognition of her as a woman means that he loved her first. But Arcite is too sensible to be persuaded by his own argument, and he drops it to fall back on one he had advanced earlier:

> Suppose that thou louedst her beforne:
> Wost thou not well the old clerkes saw
> That who shall giue a louer any law?   [A 1162–65]

Arcite's non-courtly and down-to-earth manner of speech (should one compare one's lady to a dogbone?) is redeemed by his common sense. He does not mind if Palamon loves Emily, at least from the same safe distance as he; and in the woods he seems to accept Palamon's challenge out of obligation to knighthood rather than as an opportunity to get rid of a rival. But he pulls no punches in his fighting.

The play's design assimilates Arcite to Palamon. When, in a scene by Fletcher, Palamon forbids Arcite to love Emilia because Palamon had seen her first, Arcite is allowed his rather unworthy quibble about Palamon's having mistaken her for a goddess, but is deprived of his forebear's detachment and common sense. "You shall not love at all," Palamon exclaims. "Not love at all?"

Arcite answers belligerently. "Who shall deny me?" (II.ii.165–66). When the play's Palamon, like Chaucer's before him, invokes friendship and kinship as deterrents to Arcite's loving Emilia, Arcite's reply is merely rude: "Yes, I love her. . . . If that will lose ye, farewell, Palamon"; he goes on to claim to be as "worthy and as free a lover," and to have as true a title to her as "any Palamon or any living / That is man's son (II.ii.174, 177, 178–82). Arcite's ego has been inflated to match Palamon's so that we may have a clear picture of the egotism of love destroying friendship.

Sacrificed in the play are the more thoughtful sides of both Palamon and Arcite. When Chaucer's Palamon learns of Arcite's release from prison through the intercession of Pirithous, he delivers a long soliloquy in which he expresses his envy for Arcite and then complains, most eloquently, of the cruelty of the gods who govern the world, asking them, "What is mankind more vnto you yhold / Than is the shepe that rouketh in the fold?" (A 1307–08)—an image of man as dumb beast that Shakespeare also uses.[8] The speech is part of Chaucer's complex irony, for it is Palamon whom the gods ultimately favor, though that hardly affects his charge that they are cruelly indifferent. But the play— here written by Fletcher—is interested only in Palamon's envy for Arcite, and the more thoughtful portions of the soliloquy disappear. On the same occasion, Chaucer's Arcite speaks a soliloquy in which he envies Arcite for remaining within eyeshot of Emily, from the possibility of seeing whom Arcite has been banished. Arcite is also allowed to realize wryly that only a few hours before he had been praying to be released, and now no longer wishes to be. He concludes that men do not know what they ought to pray for, for they do not know what is best for them; and he even anticipates Theseus' later conclusion that Providence may know what is good for us better than we do. Arcite comes to illustrate, ironically, his own insight, for later he prays to Mars for victory in the tournament thinking that will bring him Emily, and victory he gets, but not Emily. He dies asking, What is this world? What do men ask to have? (A 2777), having got, sadly, what he asked for. Of this ironically useless wisdom Arcite shows when he is released from prison, the play in this scene by Fletcher gives us nothing: Arcite is merely jealous of Palamon, as Palamon was of Arcite in the previous scene.

A scene (I.ii) from Shakespeare's pen wholly devoted to Palamon and Arcite is, from the point of view of characterization, one of the most disappointing scenes in the whole canon. This is a scene added to the plot, showing the two knights at home in Thebes before Theseus' expedition against Creon. They are shown to be disgusted with the decline of common morality in Thebes under King Creon, and they resolve to abandon the city. Their uninteresting dialogue suggests little more about them than that they are very moral, very innocent young men, fast friends who share a certain priggishness, perhaps more noticeable in Arcite, who is afraid of being morally contaminated by life in Thebes. But, like the good knights they are, when they hear that Theseus is at war with Thebes, they at once agree to stay and defend their city. As the scene ends, Shakespeare allows Arcite one speech that reflects the philosophical depth that Arcite in general loses in his transition from the poem to the play. Palamon wonders how they will fare in a battle in which their hearts are not in the fighting. Arcite replies,

> Let th'event,
> That never-erring arbitrator, tell us
> When we know all ourselves, and let us follow
> The becking of our chance.   [I.ii.113–16]

I have mentioned that Chaucer's Arcite anticipates Chaucer's Theseus' conclusion that Providence knows what is best for us. Here, as Edwards has pointed out, Shakespeare's Arcite anticipates the concluding speech in the play by Theseus (to which I shall return);[9] but even more strikingly, he defines the position from which Chaucer's Theseus had spoken: that is, after the event, the never-failing arbitrator, which he is now able to rationalize. Shakespeare's Arcite is allowed in this way to make his comment on the poem that Shakespeare is altering to fit new specifications, a kind of backward glance at the poem that occurs several times in the play.

If, as in *A Midsummer Night's Dream*, the male lovers in the play are even less interesting than they are in Chaucer's poem, again the loss is partly made up for in Shakespeare's characterization of a woman, Emilia. She has to receive fuller fleshing out in the play, for in the poem, as I pointed out, she is hardly more than a poetic image, a lovely object without character or individuality who speaks never a word except in her prayer to Diana before the tournament. Chaucer's Knight, indeed, does not seem to have been much of an expert on women: one feels that after his own marriage he must have stayed home just long enough to beget the Squire, and then took off for distant wars where he has been ever since, safe in the company of men. He seems to regard women as chiefly distinguished for weeping; his Theseus observes at one point that women "wepen euery in one" (A 1771), that is, continually, and all the women in *The Knight's Tale* produce a portion of tears. Only once does the Knight face Emily directly. When Arcite has won the tournament and is riding around the lists, the Knight says Emily

> ayen him cast a friendly eye
> (For women as to speake in commune
> They followen all the fauour of fortune).   [A 2680–82]

Generations of my female students have held this remark to be a cheap insult on the Knight's part, an unbecoming and infuriating slur on women. And it surely sounds cynical to say that women commonly follow fortune's favor. Yet the adaptability of women, their ability to follow fortune's favor and disfavor by making the best of even a very bad situation, is something Chaucer himself seems greatly to have admired, and it is characteristic of women as different as his Griselda and his Wife of Bath. There are indications that Shakespeare too admired this ability, for he gives some of it to his Emilia. And, indeed, I suppose that Shakespeare and Chaucer would have agreed that in the society they were describing in these works, no matter how like or unlike it may have been to their own societies, in order to survive a woman would have to be able to adapt to fortune's favor.

Like Emily, the play's more fully developed and more interesting character Emilia is forced to follow the favor of fortune, or of misfortune. As a votary of Diana, she does not want a husband, and Shakespeare goes to great lengths to show us that her not wanting one is not just a girlish whim but a sincere womanly desire. In the first scene in which she speaks at length (I.iii), she and Hippolyta are discussing the great friendship between Theseus and Pirithous, who has just left to join Theseus' expedition against Thebes. Hippolyta says something that Emilia takes as expressing anxiety that Theseus loves Pirithous more than he does his bride-to-be. Emilia tactfully, though not very confidently, reassures Hippolyta about Theseus' love. But having got on the subject of friendship between members of the same sex, Emilia tells of her own childhood love for the girl Flavina, now dead; it was so intense that Emilia now believes that "the true love 'tween maid and maid may be / More than in sex dividual." Hippolyta takes this to mean that Emilia will never love "any that's call'd man" in the way she loved Flavina, and Emilia replies, "I am sure I shall not." Hippolyta's rejoinder begins with the scorn one might expect of a bride: she calls Emilia "weak sister" with a "sickly appetite," whom one must not believe. But then she concedes that Emilia believes what she is saying, and adds most thoughtfully:

> But sure, my sister,
> If I were ripe for your persuasion, you
> Have said enough to shake me from the arm
> Of the all-noble Theseus—   [I.iii.90–91]

for whose good fortune she is going to the temple to pray, now assured, she says, that it is she and not Pirithous that Theseus loves most. This is a flagrant non-sequitur—the drift of Emilia's remarks might well have weakened rather than strengthened Hippolyta's confidence—and it perhaps suggests that Emilia has really shaken her. Emilia ends the scene with the firm declaration to Hippolyta: "I am not / Against your faith, yet I continue mine."

The scene develops the opposition of love within each sex and love between them. The friendship of Theseus and Pirithous is, of course, a model against which one may judge the destruction of the friendship of Palamon and Arcite. This much Shakespeare took over from Chaucer, where it is not emphasized. But the theme of the friendship of Theseus and Pirithous as a threat to the love of Theseus and Hippolyta is an addition, and a disturbing one, that is made even more disturbing by the mirror image provided by Emilia's description of her love for Flavina, and by her derogation of intersexual love. Edwards sees one of the large designs of the play as the necessary passage from the innocence of friendship between members of the same sex to the experience of love between the opposite sexes, and the loss that is entailed in the transition:

> [In the play] we are given, clearly enough, a life in two stages: youth, in which the passion of spontaneous friendship is dominant, and the riper age in which there is a dominant sexual passion, leading to marriage where it can. The movement from one stage to the next, the unavoidable process of growth, is a movement away from innocence, away from joy.[10]

With this fine summary I disagree in two important points. Although the play does indeed depict an unavoidable process of change, this is not necessarily growth; and though the movement is away from joy, it may not necessarily be away from innocence: it may simply be away from one experience to another that is less pleasant. Edwards is right in pointing out Shakespeare's continuing preoccupation with lost innocence; yet I do not see that the position in *The Two Noble Kinsmen* is entirely equivalent to that in *The Winter's Tale*, when Polixenes speaks of his youthful friendship for Leontes, or to that in *A Midsummer Night's Dream*, when Helena speaks of her youthful friendship for Hermia. As Clifford Leech remarks, in Emilia's talk of Flavina, "Shakespeare is no longer offering a merely gentle picture of two girls together."[11] I prefer to see what happens to Emilia as the forced exchange of one kind of experience for another. And though the friendship of the innocent Palamon and Arcite is destroyed by their love for Emilia, that love itself seems to me an expression of another kind of innocence rather than of growth. To quote Edwards' splendid image, Shakespeare "had his own dark vision to present of men moving into their future as through a thick fog."[12] Yet the future may not represent growth but merely the hardening of immaturity. As for Emilia, Shakespeare (though not Fletcher) seems to suggest that her resistance to sexual love is mature and valid, and that the entanglement of marriage is not an inevitable prescription for all women's happiness.

In *The Knight's Tale*, Emily's wishes are not consulted on any matter until, some years after the death of Arcite, Theseus asks her to marry Palamon, and even then he asks her to marry him, not if she will marry him. In the play, Emilia's wishes are consulted, but only in that she must make a cruel choice. In the scene (III. vi), written by Fletcher, in which Theseus finds the lovers fighting in the woods and sentences them to death, Emilia, like Emily, is one of the women who pray Theseus to spare them, and, in the play, it is her prayer that finally moves Theseus. He rejects, however, her suggestion that the knights be banished from his country to live separately somewhere else, a plan they reject as well. Theseus next asks Emilia to choose between them, the loser to be put to death. She refuses, though the knights agree enthusiastically. Theseus then devises the plan for a tournament between them, each supported by three knights (instead of Chaucer's hundred). The tournament itself is apparently to be non-mortal, but the losers, all four of them, will be put to death, and the winner will get Emilia. Asked if this plan contents her, she replies that it must, "Else both miscarry" (III. vi. 301). Apparently, for her to refuse to serve as prize would cause Theseus to carry out his original sentence of death on both.

Apart from one silly scene by Fletcher (IV.ii),[13] in which Emilia considers whether it is possible for her to choose one of the knights over the other—a choice the plot has suggested is no longer open to her—her part for the rest of the play is written by Shakespeare. The theme he stresses is not the possibly positive aspects of her enforced union with one of the knights, but her grief that one must die because of her. We next see her in the temple of Diana, praying to the goddess before the tournament. Her prayer differs in several ways from Emily's in *The Knight's Tale*. For Emily, the possibility of remaining a votary of Diana initially still seems real, and she prays first that she may remain unwed. She adds to her prayer, however, the wish that if she must wed one of the knights, she may wed the one who loves her best. For Emilia, faced with the prospect of marrying one knight or having both be put to death, the possibility of continuing in the service of Diana is no longer real; she is dressed as a bride, and her prayer "is the last of vestal office":

> I am bride-habited,
> But maiden-hearted. A husband I have 'pointed
> But do not know him. Out of two I should
> Choose one, and pray for his success, but I
> Am guiltless of election.   [V.i. 150–54]

I do not intend to call Emilia's sincerity into question when I point out the slight ambiguity of her statement: by refusing to choose between Palamon and Arcite she is guiltless of having made a choice of her appointed husband, and hence has broken no law of Diana. She has not, however, actually refused a husband. Perhaps afraid that Diana will be displeased with this mild quibble, she restates the issue in the negative:

> Of mine eyes
> Were I to lose one, they are equal precious.
> I could doom neither; that which perish'd should
> Go to't unsentenc'd.   [V.i. 154–56]

The choice that is offered her heart does not produce preference for one, but sorrow that either must die. In this predicament she repeats Emily's wish that the knight who loves her best should win her, but adds the request that he should also have "the truest title" to her. She is taking the advice of Chaucer's Theseus and making whatever virtue she can of necessity.

Diana's answer to Emilia teases her for a moment: the hind accompanying Emilia disappears under the altar, and "*in the place ascends a rose tree, having one rose up on it.*" Seeing this Emilia wonders whether

> this battle shall confound
> Both these brave knights, and I, a virgin flow'r,
> Must grow alone, unpluck'd.   [V.i. 166–68]

But the rose falls from the tree and Emilia knows she must not remain unplucked. Her use of *must* is charming, as if, though she wishes to remain unwed, after all these elaborate preparations it might be too sudden a reversal of fortune's favor if she did. But as from the earlier scene between Hippolyta and Emilia, one comes away with a strong sense that Diana's appeal has its own large validity. The goddess's chilly charm is marvelously invoked by Emilia at the beginning of her prayer:

> O sacred, shadowy, cold, and constant queen,
> Abandoner of revels, mute, contemplative,
> Sweet, solitary, white as chaste, and pure
> As wind-fann'd snow. . . .   V.i.137–40]

Emilia does not follow her marital fortune with enthusiasm. Despite the urging of Hippolyta and Theseus—the virtual command of the latter—she refuses to watch the tournament. Her thoughts are always with the loser, and what her Martian sister and brother-in-law regard as a wonderful opportunity to see brave deeds done in her honor she regards as a punishment. When, with the tournament in progress, she is left alone, she does, for the first time in Shakespeare's handling of her, consider the relative excellence of the two knights, but can bring herself to prefer neither (V.iii.41–104). Her mind constantly returns to the fact that one must die. When she hears shouts suggesting that Palamon is winning, her first thought is of Arcite: "Poor servant, thou hast lost." And when she hears that it is Arcite who has won, she praises his excellence, but concludes, "Alas, poor Palamon!" One wonders whether, if she had been placed in a situation in which she was forced to choose one, with the other going free, she would not have chosen Arcite. But the position she is in ensures the death of one man, which no choice of hers can prevent.

That she finds herself in this cruel position is the result of the edict by Theseus, who is much altered from what he was in Chaucer. The earlier Theseus, though he takes most seriously the responsibility of imposing his idea of order on the unruly world, and shows himself at times to be both hotheaded and ruthless, has both humor and tolerance, and an ability to entertain second thoughts. But from the very first scene of the play, when the widowed queens importune him for aid, Shakespeare's Theseus appears as a harsher, more remote, more prideful, more bullheaded figure than his forebear. The latter is at first angered by the procession of queens interrupting his triumphant home-coming, and accuses them of envy of his honor; but when he learns who they are and what they want, he at once accedes to their request and leads his army against Thebes (A 905–74). Shakespeare's Theseus, though he shows sympathy for the wid-owed queens, has no intention of deferring his marriage festivi-ties on their behalf. The fact that he and Hippolyta are still un-married, as in *A Midsummer Night's Dream*, gives Theseus some reason for his behavior, though it is a reason that illustrates the debilitating power of Venus on civilized behavior. Theseus says that he considers his forthcoming marriage "greater than any war," adding

> It more imports me
> Than all the actions that I have foregone,
> Or futurely can cope.   [I.i. 172–74]

Apparently this Theseus has never toyed with Ariadne's affec-tions or been assisted in his amours by Titania. But even if this marriage is a novel experience for him and one of great urgency, his refusal to aid the queens until their cause has been eloquently pleaded by Hippolyta and Emilia makes him seem like a cold and self-centered person. If this is Venus' power at work, then it isolates him from humanity, as it does Palamon and Arcite. The impression of his isolation is reinforced by such speeches as that in which he tells the widow of King Capaneus how "grief and time" have withered her beauty (I.i. 59–70), which he remem-bers from her wedding. He seems a living statue of Mars, un-touchable by human feelings.

In almost every scene in which he appears, the play's Theseus surpasses his Chaucerian predecessor in expressing his power and ruthlessness. He greatly admires the way Palamon and Ar-cite fought against him in the battle at Thebes, and when he finds them wounded on the field, he instructs his herald to em-ploy the best doctors in Athens to heal their injuries. But this apparent bit of humanity is spoiled when he gloats over the fact that he has them in his power, the power of life and death. In Chaucer, the political necessity to imprison the knights is simply taken for granted. Shakespeare's Theseus makes the knights' excellence contribute to the pride he has in being their captor:

> their lives concern us
> Much more than Thebes is worth. Rather than have 'em
> Freed of this plight, and in their morning state
> (Sound and at liberty), I would 'em dead;
> But forty thousand fold we had rather have 'em
> Prisoners to us than death. [I.iv.32–37]

There is in this speech the same stench of sickness that there is in *Troilus and Cressida* when Achilles feels Hector's limbs and admires the strength that he intends to destroy.

There is some uncertainty over whether the last scene I was discussing in *The Two Noble Kinsmen* is Shakespeare's or Fletcher's,[14] but on Theseus the two playwrights agree, each emphasizing his ruthlessness. It may have been Fletcher who decided that the order should be given, presumably by Theseus, that Palamon be moved to a more remote part of the prison after Arcite's release, with the result that Palamon could no longer see Emilia, a gratuitous touch of cruelty. Like Chaucer's, Fletcher's Theseus condemns Palamon and Arcite to death at once when he finds them fighting in the woods (III.vi); but unlike Chaucer's Theseus, who changes his mind after the ladies' intercession and his own charming meditation on the absurdity of lovers (A 1742–1825), the Theseus of the play once again yields most reluctantly to others' entreaties, and finally gives in only because he had once promised Emilia that he would grant her anything she wanted. He had given his word that the knights would be put to death, and he apparently thinks that their death is less important than keeping his word. We recall that, in Chaucer, Venus was able to keep her word to Palamon by the death of Arcite: Theseus is imitating the arbitrariness of the Chaucerian immortals.

The play's Theseus is excessively touchy about chivalric honor, and thinks that any knight should be as touchy as he. He assumes, without making inquiry, that not only the loser in the tournament between Palamon and Arcite, but also the loser's three companions would rather be put to death than to go on living after the defeat, a curious notion by which he makes honor responsible for increasing man's inhumanity to man.[15] At the last minute, Chaucer's Theseus forbids the use of certain lethal weapons in the tournament in order to reduce the danger of death to the contestants (A 2537–60). Shakespeare's Theseus, on the other hand, ensures the death of half of the contestants. He is mercilessly all-or-nothing, Venus or Mars, love or death. When Arcite wins the tournament, Shakespeare's Theseus awards Emilia to him and in the same breath says of the four defeated knights, "Give them our present justice, since I know / Their lives but pinch them" (V.iii.132–33). This seems a curious use of the word *justice*; nor is it clear that the knights' lives do pinch them. Palamon faces impending execution with graceful stoicism—not quite the same thing as enthusiasm—and uses a part of the consolation that Chaucer's Theseus had used to stop Emily and Palamon from mourning Arcite's death: that is, it is well to die when one is innocent of wrong and, so to speak, ahead of the game, before age brings moral or physical corruption (V.iv.1–14; cf. A 3047–56). But one does not feel that, if Theseus had suddenly and uncharacteristically reversed himself, Palamon and his companions would have insisted that the sentence be carried out.

Shakespeare's Theseus, Palamon and Arcite, and Hippolyta all represent Mars come down from the temple walls in Chaucer and into their hearts. They control their world by the sword alone. But of course, as Edwards has so clearly shown, Venus is a danger to human behavior, and no less a one than Mars. At the end of the first scene Theseus realizes he has hesitated to help the widowed queens because of his eagerness for Venerean pursuits, admitting, in a moment of self-awareness that I wish he would have more often, that "being sensually subdu'd [that is, overcome by sensuality], / We lose our human title" (I.i.232–33). The fight that is maintained between Palamon and Arcite because of Venus' influence deprives them of humanity. Their eagerness to kill one another in claiming the right to love Emilia—or, in the scene by Fletcher loosely based on Chaucer, to be put to death rather than to stop fighting for that right—is both superhuman and subhuman. And, of course, the destructive power of Venus is the chief motif illustrated by the subplot of the jailer's daughter, handled almost exclusively by Fletcher, and hence not included in my discussion. This subplot also introduces the theme of the exchangeability of lovers, implicit in *The Knight's Tale* and developed in *A Midsummer Night's Dream.* Love's exchangeability is not a motif that adds to Venus' stature.

Since Palamon and Arcite are equally dedicated to love and fighting, to Venus and Mars, it is only symmetry that demands that one must be a votary of one of the gods, and the other of the other. Even in Chaucer, Arcite's assignment to Mars seems arbitrary, for Palamon is actually the more quarrelsome of the two. Chaucer did what he could to smoothe over the arbitrariness by having Arcite, in his prayer, remind Mars of his liaison with Venus, which her husband Vulcan had so embarrassingly publicized. But the real reason that Arcite had to pray to Mars in the older form of the story was that he had to fulfill his character by praying for the wrong thing, victory instead of Emily (A 2420). This is a relatively minor need in Shakespeare's version of the story, from which such ironies have been eradicated. The prayer his Arcite makes is straightforward bloody praise of the god: Emilia is the prize that must be "dragg'd out of blood" (V.i.43) and, hence, Arcite needs Mars's help.

But the ugliness of Arcite's prayer to Mars (earlier I gave a specimen of its ugliness) is surpassed by the ugliness of Palamon's prayer to Venus—the most amazing passage in the play, from any point of view. It is as if Palamon had studied the wall paintings in Venus' temple in *The Knight's Tale* and decided that she was to be praised most for her ability to corrupt or make fools of men of any age. His most striking image is that of the senile lover, "the poll'd bachelor" whom Venus can catch at seventy

> And make him, to the scorn of his hoarse throat,
> Abuse young lays of love.   [V.i.88–89]

One thinks of *The Merchant's Tale*—how in the morning old January "chaunteth" and "cracketh" to May while the "slacke skin about his necke shaketh" (E 1849–50). What part of Palamon's prayer is not devoted to Venus' power to humiliate and corrupt is devoted to praise of himself for never having conspired sexually against women or made lewd jokes about them, constantly reminding himself, like a good boy, that he had a mother. But even this prim protestation is modified by his story of having himself known an eighty-year-old man whose fourteen-year-old wife had given birth to a boy, and by his claim that he, Palamon, believed the child was the husband's because the wife had sworn it was. Either Palamon is unbelievably innocent or his account of this marvel comes very close to the kind of joking he boasts he has eschewed. In any case, his praise of the goddess is almost wholly for her power to debase. He does not mention the strife she has caused between himself and Arcite, but then no character in the play apart from Emilia seems to have the self-awareness that such an admission would require.

Palamon gets Emilia, and is snatched from the jaws of death to do so. Arcite, having won the tournament and having been awarded Emilia, rides around the city on a horse Emilia had given him (an irony that the play adds to the story), and Pirithous describes to the astounded Palamon the off-stage accident in which Arcite is mortally injured. In Chaucer it is a fury sent by Pluto at Saturn's request on behalf of Venus that causes the horse to rear in such a way that Arcite's breast is smashed against the saddlebow (A 2684–91). In Shakespeare we do not know what gods, if any, were involved. Arcite's horse is frightened by a spark caused by its own hooves, and Saturn has been reduced to a part of an image: Pirithous does not know

> what envious flint,
> Cold as old Saturn, and like him possess'd
> With fire malevolent,   [V.iv.61–63]

raised the spark that frightened the horse so that it reared and fell backward upon its rider.

In *The Knight's Tale*, Arcite takes a long time a-dying, and an even longer time being buried in the splendid funeral Theseus arranges for him. Years pass before Theseus summons Palamon back from Thebes and marries him off to Emily, after delivering his sententious speech on the operation of Divine Providence.

The equivalent action in *The Two Noble Kinsmen* takes but a few minutes, fifty-two lines as opposed to more than five hundred in the poem. All but sixteen lines of the play's scene in which Arcite delivers his dying speech and Emilia is forthwith transferred to Palamon are assigned to Theseus. In Chaucer's corresponding scene, Theseus argues that because we are governed by a divine plan—for whose existence he provides no evidence—it is "wisdome"

> To make vertue of necessite
> And take it well that we may not eschew.   [A 3042–43]

But, again, he does not argue that the divine plan corresponds to man's idea of justice, that Palamon deserved Emily more than Arcite, or that Arcite deserved death; what he argues is that it is most economical, as it were, to take what comes with good grace. The wisdom of being prepared for anything in a world where chance seems to rule supreme had earlier been asserted by the Knight himself (A 1523–24). But the play has no such thoughtful message; it has, indeed, no moral, except that the world dominated by Mars and Venus is a messy one: nor, as I have said, are Mars and Venus objective figures as in *The Knight's Tale*, but merely human impulses objectified only in a poetic image. Theseus does try to find some higher principle at work. He feels that in Arcite's accident things have come out for the best, and Arcite himself asserts the same principle: Arcite admits that he was "false" to Palamon, "yet never treacherous" (V.iv.92–93)—a distinction so fine as to be scarcely visible. What this does is allow Arcite to die with his chivalry virtually unsullied, while allowing Palamon's claim to Emilia to have been just. Theseus is delighted with the opportunity offered him to promote the quibble that Palamon had seen Emilia first into a legal principle asserting Palamon's better title. With equal regard for niceties if not substantials, Theseus also observes that the "deities / Have show'd due justice" (V.iv.108–09), in that Mars and Venus kept their promises of success to their two votaries—that this includes a classic example of divine equivocation is not mentioned. But because Theseus has always thought of human action in the simplified terms of the alternatives of love or death, in the world in which he lives justice has indeed triumphed. Indeed, the death of Arcite and the good fortune of Palamon even enable Theseus to perform a humane act—he calls off the execution of Palamon's companions in arms. As he observes,

> The gods my justice
> Take from my hand, and they themselves become
> The executioners, [V.iv.120–22]

and more merciful ones than he, I might add.

Shakespeare must have been aware that his play, unlike Chaucer's poem, was not about the chance-laden interaction of gods and mortals; yet he allows Theseus to pretend that it was, and gives him a final address to the gods which would splendidly become Chaucer's Theseus in Chaucer's poem:

> O you heavenly charmers,
> What things you make of us! For what we lack
> We laugh, for what we have are sorry, still
> Are children in some kind. Let us be thankful
> For that which is, and with you leave dispute
> That are above our question. [V.iv.131–36]

But against this graceful affirmation and acceptance of things as they are, one still hears in one's mind a speech Emilia made just as Theseus awarded her to the triumphant Arcite, whom he told to "arm [his] prize." The prize addresses the gods:

> O all you heavenly powers, where is your mercy?
> But that your wills have said it must be so,
> And charge me live to comfort this unfriended,
> This miserable prince, that cuts away
> A life more worthy from him than all women,
> I should and would die too. [V.iii.139–44]

The heavenly powers that Emilia addresses are of course in the hearts of Theseus, of Hippolyta, of Palamon, and of Arcite, and it is their wills that have said it must be so. Edwards finds in *The Two Noble Kinsmen* some of the same "irony of the way in which [Palamon and Arcite's] course is shaped by chance and coincidence" that exists in *The Knight's Tale*,[16] but it seems to me that in the play it is actually only Emilia who is helpless before chance in the same sense that the heroes of *The Knight's Tale* are. What is in Chaucer the disastrous folly of their courtship, an aspect of their youth, becomes in the play the index of their mature characters: they become fully Martian-Venerean, and no further growth can occur in a world willing to settle unquestioningly for such second-rate deities.

Emilia does question the principles of such a world. Her description of herself as having to go on living in order to comfort a husband wretched in the loss of a friend who was more worthy than any woman is maidenly-modest to a high degree; nevertheless, its very modesty reiterates Emilia's earlier statement that, for her, friendship between persons of the same sex is of a higher quality than love between the sexes. It is no mere self-deprecation when she says that Arcite has lost more in Palamon than he could ever find compensation for in Emilia. The sudden reversal of the situation, with Arcite dead and Emilia transferred to Palamon, rather than changing an iota of the sense of Emilia's speech, reinforces its validity. She could speak in the new situation just as she spoke in the old, and she could begin her speech by addressing to the triumphant Palamon, as she had to the triumphant Arcite, the question that provides an excellent if oblique commentary on the play: "Is this winning?" In its questioning of the way things are, Emilia's living despair in *The Two Noble Kinsmen* is as poignant as the dying Arcite's despair in *The Knight's Tale* when he asks,

What is the world? What asken men to haue?   [A 2777]

4

Criseyde Becoming Cressida:
Troilus and Criseyde and
Troilus and Cressida

hen in Shakespeare's *Troilus and Cressida* Ulysses utters his famous condemnation of Cressida,

> Fie, fie upon her!
> There's language in her eye, her cheek, her lip,
> Nay, her foot speaks; her wanton spirits look out
> At every joint and motive of her body, [IV. v. 54–57][1]

he seems to be responding to one of Chaucer's narrator's not very informative descriptions of Criseyde in the first book of his poem about the lovers:

> She nas nat with the most of her stature,
> But all her limmes so well answering
> Weren to womanhode, that creature
> Was neuer lasse manissh in seming;
> And eke the pure wise of her meaning
> Shewed wel that men might in her gesse
> Honour, estate, and womanly noblesse. [I 281–87][2]

Ulysses has apparently been reading Chaucer, but he is not one of those men who Chaucer says may, on the basis of the way Criseyde-Cressida looks, guess that she possesses honor, estate, and womanly noblesse: if Shakespeare could read through the meaningless word "meaning" in the black-letter text back to Chaucer's original *meving*, "moving," then Ulysses in using the word *motive* may be directly alluding to Chaucer. In any case, the way Cressida looks and moves bespeaks for Ulysses a slut; and he thinks old Nestor, who has just remarked admiringly that she is "a woman of quick sense," is silly not to recognize her for what she is.

The two quotations dramatize the problem of the relation of Shakespeare's heroine to Chaucer's. The two women are artistic realizations of the same legendary figure, but they have very dissimilar personalities, so dissimilar that some scholars have denied that Chaucer's Criseyde had any significant influence on Shakespeare's Cressida: one usually excellent critic denied that Shakespeare had read Chaucer's poem.[3] However, one scholar, John Bayley, has wondered aloud whether the two women "are not in fact based on the same kind of interest and understanding on the part of the two writers; and even whether Shakespeare, with that sureness of instinct which makes it irrelevant to ask whether or not he was 'interested' in such a character, may not have formed his Cressida from Chaucer's."[4] I think that is precisely what Shakespeare did. In this chapter I shall talk about Shakespeare's Cressida in the light of Chaucer's Criseyde— rather than in the darkness cast by her shadow, as is too often done.

Because I assume that Shakespeare had a profound understanding of Chaucer's poem, I shall first have to get rid of a school of red herrings that has been strewn across the path of anyone hunting for Chaucer's Criseyde in Shakespeare's Cressida. Shakespeare read Chaucer's *Troilus* in Thynne's edition of Chaucer's works of 1532, or one of its reprintings of 1542 or 1550, in Stow's edition of 1561, or in Speght's edition of 1598.[5] In all of these the text of *Troilus*—essentially the same text in all—is somewhat corrupt, though not as corrupt as that of *The Canterbury Tales*. And in all of them Robert Henryson's poem, *The Testament of Cresseid*, is printed after the end of the last book of Chaucer's *Troilus*, with no indication of change in authorship. This work, written about a century after Chaucer's poem, concerns the later history of Chaucer's heroine, describing how, cast off by Diomeid, for whom she had abandoned Troilus, she became a leper and, the poet suggests, a whore: leprosy in the later Middle Ages was generally considered a venereal disease. It has frequently been suggested—indeed, in some quarters it has become an article of faith—that, because of the corruption of the printed text, much of the richness and subtlety of Chaucer's poem would have been lost to Shakespeare, who would not have recognized him fully for the great poet he is; and because of the appearance of Henryson's *Testament* in a volume entitled *The Works of Chaucer*, Shakespeare would have received a highly distorted notion of Chaucer's heroine.[6] To quote the well-known article of 1917 in which Heider Rollins traces the "deterioration" of Criseyde's character from Chaucer's time to Shakespeare's: "it is almost certain that Shakespeare thought [*The Testament*] to be Chaucer's own work."[7]

I shall attempt to dispose of these arguments one by one. In the first place, though the printed text of Chaucer's *Troilus* is indeed corrupt from an editor's point of view, it is seldom so poor as to interfere with the understanding of even a moderately attentive reader, which I suppose Shakespeare to have been. The reading of *meaning* for *meving* is one of two corruptions in the stanza I quoted, and while it takes the edge off my point about the relation of Ulysses' speech to Chaucer, it hardly interferes with Chaucer's general sense. I don't know what Shakespeare took the pure wise of Criseyde's *meaning* to look like, but I'm sure he knew it was lovely. The other corruption is in the statement that Criseyde was not with the most of her stature: Chaucer wrote *least*, but I think in either case we end up with middle-sized. In all respects, the description of Criseyde as printed is wholly intelligible.

But as important to how Shakespeare understood Chaucer is the matter of Henryson. It seems to me that to suppose that Shakespeare thought Chaucer wrote *The Testament* is to attribute to him not only little Latin and less Greek, but minimal English and no sense. The colophon at the end of Chaucer's poem in the black-letter editions announces, "Thus endeth the fifth booke, and laste of Troylus: and here foloweth the pitefull and dolorous Testament of faire Creseide." "The testament of Creseide" is the running head for Henryson's poem, setting it apart from "The first [etc.] Booke of Troilus." The *Testament* itself begins with the introduction of what the dullest reader must recognize as a different narrator from the one who has just finished his poem with a splendid prayer, and a narrator speaking a different dialect of English. This narrator, in order to warm himself up on a cold night, takes down from his bookshelf not a book, but a *queare*,

> Writen by worthy Chaucer glorious
> Of faire Criseide and lusty Troilus.   [41–42][8]

He summarizes the sad end of Chaucer's poem in two stanzas, omitting any mention of Troilus's death. A third stanza begins,

> Of his [Troilus's] distresse me nedeth nat reherse
> For worthy Chaucer in that same boke
> In goodly termes and in ioly verse
> Compiled hath his cares, who wil loke.   [57–60]

Then, in order "to breke [his] sleep," the narrator takes down another *queare* containing "the fatal destiny / Of faire Creseide, which ended wretchedly." The next stanza begins with the question, "Who wote if al that Chaucer wrate was trew?" after which the narrator goes on to admit that he doesn't know if this other narrative is "authorized or forged[9] of the new" by some poet using his own invention. I very much doubt that Shakespeare after reading this and later encountering alive and well Troilus, whom Chaucer had left in Mercury's hands up in the seventh sphere,[10] could have supposed that he was reading anything "authorized" by Chaucer, regardless of his volume's title page. No, this composite Henry Chaucerson simply will not do: imagine Chaucer allowing any of his narrators to refer to their creator as "worthy Chaucer glorious!"[11]

The Henryson canard is an integral part of the theory that, in creating his Cressida, Shakespeare was a victim of literary determinism: that is, because Henryson and his numerous imitators, both respectable poets and ballad-makers, had made nasty remarks about the Cressid figure, her literary character had so deteriorated by Shakespeare's time that there was nothing he could do but present a thoroughly malodorous Cressida, even if he had wanted to do otherwise.[12] This is said about a playwright who, having made a tragedy out of the happily ending story of

Lear and a living statue of a dead Hermione, and presented two totally different Theseuses and Hippolytas, does not seem to have been very anxious to keep literary history flowing in its predetermined course. Shakespeare could surely have done any-thing he wished with Cressida—even made her faithful, as Dry-den did, though thank heaven he didn't wish that. But this theory, aside from underrating Shakespeare's potential for orig-inality, has a more vicious result in that, while purporting to explain after the fact why Cressida is an unattractive character, it works equally well to force the reader to find her unattractive; that is, if for historical reasons Shakespeare could not make Cressida attractive, she must be unattractive.[13] Unfortunately, literary determinism has a powerful effect on Shakespearean critics regardless of whether it had any effect on Shakespeare, and one sometimes encounters critics who insist that it is wrong to try to defend Shakespeare's Cressida as a person, because his-torically she is indefensible.

The theory of Criseyde's deterioration between Chaucer's and Shakespeare's time has the effect of blurring several other im-portant issues. It tends to ignore, for instance, the very impor-tant fact that, whereas it is perfectly possible to defend either one as a person, Criseyde's or Cressida's behavior with Troilus has always been, in the long run, indefensible. Yet reading com-parisons of Shakespeare's heroine with Chaucer's one often feels that Chaucer's heroine was somehow a better and more moral unfaithful woman than Shakespeare's, a nice girl sadly gone wrong, rather than just a tart, though they behave in exactly the same way.[14] I hope I am not imposing my own literary deter-minism on Shakespeare when I insist that he chose to re-create Cressida because she was the prototypical unfaithful woman. Benoît de Sainte Maure, who invented her, used her as an excuse to spew out misogyny (in a book dedicated, rather tactlessly, to a lady), and the misogyny sounds even worse in Guido della Colonne's Latin translation of Benoît.[15] It is said that Boccaccio intended his Criseida to represent his hotly loved mistress, Maria d'Aquino, apparently in revenge for an infidelity she was guilty of or one he knew she would be guilty of. And no matter how much charm Chaucer's Criseyde shows in the course of her

love affair with Troilus, she betrays him brutally in the end. Indeed, Thersites' comment in Shakespeare's play on Cressida's
last soliloquy, in which she admits to following the error of her
eyes, is as just a comment on Criseyde as on Cressida, and on
all the Cressid-kind:

> A proof of strength she could not publish more,
> Unless she said, "My mind is now turn'd whore." [V.ii.113–14]

This is exactly what Criseyde's mind is doing in her long speech
to Diomede in Book V (956–1008), in which she keeps one eye
on Troy and one on him.

What more appropriate heroine could there be for a play, one
of whose major themes is human inconstancy and inconsistency,[16] than the woman whose name had become a synonym
for inconstancy? The play is full of passionate statements of ideals which are then ignored by the very characters who stated
them. Every man in the play, except Pandarus and Thersites,
who are unburdened by ideals, is inconsistent: Troilus, at first
rendered by love too woman-weak to fight, fighting a moment
later, and by the end of the play fighting, and urging Hector to
fight, like a merciless madman; in council arguing that the Trojans should keep Helen because one must at all costs hold on to
the things one values, and then making no effort to prevent
Cressida's transfer to the Greek camp; Hector, splendidly arguing that Helen must be returned to the Greeks and then abruptly
turning his back on his own argument; later allowing a whim-
sical desire for a suit of gold armor to obliterate both his chivalry and his prudence; Achilles, the great martial hero, playing
silly games in his tent with Patroclus, refusing to fight even after
he has undertaken to, and when he finally fights fighting like a
coward; and Ulysses, whose assumed horror at Patroclus' in-
subordinate mockery of Agamemnon and Nestor is thoroughly
tainted by the petty delight he takes in telling Agamemnon and
Nestor about the mockery; who discourses magnificently on
human behavior and behaves himself like a second-rate, incom-
petent Machiavel. For a world in which virtues blaze up, sputter,
and then go out, what better symbol could there be than the
Cressida of literary tradition? In her inconsistency she is in ex-

cellent company; Alexander's description to her of Ajax in the play's second scene is a not unapt description of almost everyone concerned: "There is no man hath a virtue that he [Ajax] hath not a glimpse of, nor any man an attaint but he carries some stain of it" (I.ii. 24–26).

Chaucer's great achievement with Criseyde is to invoke so much sympathy for her in the earlier part of the poem that her foreknown act of betrayal comes as a shock to the reader—not unlike the shock of tragedy—when what his mind has known all along will happen happens against the expectation of his heart. This sympathy for Criseyde is mostly produced by Chaucer's narrator, who, being head over heels in love with her, suffuses his characterization of her with adoration.[17] For the most part of four books, all propositions relating to her—her appearance, her behavior, her motives—whether the propositions are self-evidently true or wholly dubious, are relayed to us with loving approbation. She does indeed have attractive qualities that we can perceive without the narrator's having to work over-time—gaiety, grace, elegance, some humor—in short, much female charm—but many of our sympathetic responses to her are actually responses to the narrator's manipulation of her and us. Although she is surely in a precarious position in a Troy to which her father has turned traitor, the narrator's introduction of her is more emotional than candid: we meet her, poor thing, in peril from an outraged Trojan populace, "all alone, / And [she] nist to whom she might make her mone" (I.97–98).[18] Who will not pity so forlorn a creature, who also happens to be, according to the fourteenth-century narrator's own eyewitness, the loveliest woman in all ancient Troy? And so we pity her, and gladly forgive both her and her narrator when it turns out that, far from being all alone and knowing no one to whom she might complain, she has a couple of nieces and a dozen or so attendant women residing with her in what is later referred to as a palace, and an uncle who often drops in for a chat and in whom she confides. Somehow we are made to feel that this comfortable environment is the proper one for so elegant a damsel in distress to enjoy her distress in.

Out of respect for Chaucer's celebrated insight into the human psyche I should like to credit him with having created a woman we can fully understand as well as love. But the fact is that, while the narrator at times seems to be cramming us with information about her, he succeeds in giving us remarkably few firm facts. From the description I quoted earlier, for instance, we learn that, though she was not among the largest (Chaucer wrote smallest) of women, all her limbs so well answered to womanhood that no one ever seemed less masculine—a collection of data from which it is hard to infer much. An earlier description in Book I tells us helpfully that her native beauty was so angel-like that she seemed an immortal thing, such as a heavenly perfect creature that might be sent down in scorn of nature—an angel, perhaps? (I 100–05). A third description is unhelpful in a different way: in the temple where Troilus first notices her, Criseyde, in black, though no one ever saw so bright a star under a black cloud, is standing full low, and still, alone, behind other people, a little apart, and near the door, under dread of shame, simple of attire, meek of expression— with fully assured look and manner; and some lines later, when Troilus gazes at her, this timid creature lets her look fall a little aside, as if to say, "What, may I not stand here?" (I 169–82, 288–92).

In fact, Chaucer's narrator gives us precious little information about Criseyde, and when he does give some, it is often like the last description, paradoxical and ambiguous. What he does is present us with the portrait of a woman of almost mythological femininity, and readers respond to such a portrait by becoming their own mythmakers, working on those aspects of Criseyde they find most congenial. And what an abundance of contradictory qualities we have to work on! Criseyde is the timidest creature in the world, afraid of Greeks, and of love, and of steel weapons; she is also, as we have just seen, of full assured looking and manner, and she almost never loses her poise or self-possession; she trembles like an aspen leaf in Troilus's embrace, a poor lark in the clutches of a sparrow hawk, to whom, a few minutes before, she has had to administer first aid for a fainting fit. Indeed, in the details of carrying on a love affair a certain aggressiveness compromises her timidity. Initially she asks Pan-

darus whether Troilus can speak well of love, but when, on their
first night together, Troilus goes on and on speaking well of it,
she finally interrupts:

> But let vs fall away fro this mattere,
> For it suffiseth, this that said is here,
> And at o word, without repentaunce,
> Welcome, my knight, my peace, my suffisaunce.   [III 1306–09]

Despite the strong impression readers are given by the narrator
that she is a modest, chaste widow, she observes, on the first
occasion that Troilus rides by her window after she has learned
that he loves her, that he has both "a bodie and might / To
doen" an unspecified "thing" (II 633–34)—an observation at
which she blushes. And, as I mentioned before, when it appears
that the lovers are going to waste their last night together in
lamentation on the floor, she suggests that they rise and go
straight to bed. Criseyde never forgets that lovemaking and
speechmaking must yield courteously and timely to one another.

Her occasionally forward behavior provides materials to
those readers who wish to find in Criseyde prognostications of
her future actions;[19] and that Chaucer was anxious to provide
such materials appears from his occasionally allowing his narrator to engender suspicion of Criseyde in attempting to quell it.
Thus when, in Book II, she is considering whether to accept
Troilus as a lover, the narrator suddenly intrudes to scold any
reader who thinks she is falling in love too fast—a possibility
that, in view of her painstaking deliberateness, few readers
would have entertained if the narrator had not mentioned it. Of
course, once a reader has become suspicious, even the most innocent statements about Criseyde become suspect. Thus such
seemingly laudatory comments as the narrator's "For she was
wise" (III 86), or reports of her inner thoughts such as "It nedeth
me ful slighly for to pley" (II 462), have struck some readers as
sinister betrayals of the romance-heroine's obligation to be as
thoughtless as she is beautiful, and lead to suggestions that she
is, like her father Calchas, calculating.

Perhaps the best example of the technique of ambiguity that

Chaucer uses with Criseyde occurs when, in the small chamber at Deiphobus' house, Pandarus is urging her to take pity on the bedridden Troilus. Her response is thus described:

> With that she gan her eyen on him cast
> Full easily and full debonairly,
> Auising her, and hied nat to fast
> With neuer a worde.   [III 155–58]

"Hied nat to fast": did not hurry too fast. The suspicious reader will hear the verb *hied* and have his impression confirmed that she is indeed hurrying, but, for appearance's sake, not too fast, and his suspicion may be reinforced by the phrase "Auising her," keeping her mind in control of the situation. The sympathetic reader, on the other hand, will understand the words to mean that Criseyde is proceeding at precisely the right modest speed expected of a heroine whom one wishes to see give in, but not too fast; such a reader will congratulate her on her good sense in looking before she leaps. Chaucer would be happy with either impression, and happier with both, though his narrator would be horrified at the first. For here he is, crediting his heroine with the ability to execute that impossible maxim, *festina lente*, "make haste slowly." As I have said elsewhere,[20] most members of the human race simply cannot festinate with lentitude—only Chaucer's myth of lovely femininity, his not unimpossible she, could pull it off.

At the end of this scene in Deiphobus' house Criseyde accepts Troilus as her "servant", though with strictly defined limitations, and perhaps even stricter undefined ones. But she makes her first move toward him unprodded (for once) by Pandarus, and in a splendidly generous speech she promises to turn Troilus' bitter into sweet and

> "If I be she that may do you gladnesse
> For euery wo ye shall recouer a blisse,"
> And him in armes toke, and gan him kisse.   [III 180–82]

We who have read the poem before know that it was a long time after this before Criseyde accepted Troilus into her bed—a long but totally undefined time—so that we understand that when

here she took Troilus in her arms and *gan* him kiss, she merely
did kiss him, perhaps once, sisterly; on the other hand, it is impossible to distinguish in Chaucer between *gan* as the auxiliary
"did" and *gan* as the verb "began": either she did kiss him, or
else she began to kiss him, and continued, until, a full stanza
later, Pandarus, who has been on his knees for seven lines thanking Cupid and Venus, interrupts with, "But ho, no more now
of this mattere!" (III 190). Even in the clearest, most straightforward accounts of Criseyde's behavior, ambiguity intrudes.

It is a principle in physics that transparent bodies refract part
of the light incident upon them and reflect another part. I suppose it is unfair to liken to a transparent body someone I have
just presented as something of a blur, but Criseyde's qualities
appear both refracted and reflected in Shakespeare's Cressida.
John Bayley believes that what the two women "chiefly have in
common is that neither of them know what they want, and so
they both become victims of what other people want."[21] This is
a shrewd observation, though it seems to me to apply rather
better to Criseyde than to Cressida. Nor does it take sufficiently
into account that there is something both of them want and
want desperately, Cressida more than Criseyde because she has
less of it: that is security from the perils of life in Troy. I think
Shakespeare was particularly struck by the vulnerability of
Chaucer's heroine, her precariousness, as the daughter of a traitor, in a city at war. He even adds to her precariousness by suggesting that Calchas has made a number of unsuccessful attempts to transfer his daughter from Troy to the Greek camp
before the play begins.[22] I'm sure Shakespeare was not fooled by
Chaucer's narrator's misleading introduction of Criseyde as all
alone and not knowing to whom she might complain, but he
adopts its suggestion for the predicament in which to place his
Cressida. War is a far more real presence in his play, and Cressida is not a well-to-do widow with a large household and much
female companionship. Rather, she is a young, unmarried
woman, presumably with a house, though not one that gives
the impression of stability and ease imparted by Criseyde's
paved parlor, gold-embroidered cushions, garden with sanded
paths, and, above all, attendant women. Cressida is one of

Shakespeare's few unmarried women without a confidante—no Celia, no Nerissa, not even a Nurse. Miranda at least has a wise if somewhat grumpy father.

But poor Cressida has no one to confide in but Pandarus, in whom she does not confide, for he is a very seedy uncle compared to Criseyde's, and one intent on serving her up on a platter to his friend Prince Troilus. In this last respect he resembles his forerunner, but the danger to Cressida is far greater because she is already in love with the man he is trying to serve her up to. Cressida's infatuation with Troilus before the action begins is perhaps Shakespeare's most radical alteration in the love story. Much of the leisurely development of Criseyde's character in Chaucer occurs not when she is in love but when she is deciding whether she will accept the service of a man with whom she may, in some remote future, fall in love, if she feels like it. Presumably she accepts Troilus as a servant at Deiphobus' house at the beginning of Book III, but, as I have said, it was long before she admitted him to intimacy, and one gets the impression that she finally slid into love rather than falling into it: her progress lacks urgency. But with Cressida love is not merely an alternative lifestyle, something one is free to accept or reject; it is a fact of her young life, and one that both hurts and frightens. We have only to watch Rosalind—or, for more extreme examples, either Helena—to see the unnerving effect falling in love has on even Shakespeare's nicest heroines; and they at least have the comfort of hoping they may wind up with a husband, not just a lover, which seems to be the most a Trojan girl can expect.

That, from the very beginning of the play, Cressida is not a nice girl is a proposition that seems to have great appeal for moralistic critics, who find even so natural an act as her having fallen in love—and at first sight!—proof of her innate light-mindedness.[23] Though she has never been without defenders, until recently the weightiest critics of the play seem to have been followers of Ulysses, the first high-minded intellectual to settle Cressida's business by calling her a slut.[24] At least he is terse about it, whereas some of her modern non-admirers go on at great length demonstrating the badness of her character, as if they felt obligated to stop the reader from wasting his emotions

on the wrong kind of woman. Such preoccupation with establishing Cressida's sluttishness seems to reflect a kind of emotional involvement with her that is less literary than personal.
Like the stern parents of a bad Victorian girl in a bad Victorian
novel, critics turn Cressida's picture to the wall, on which they
leave it ostentatiously hanging, dramatizing at once their disapproval of her and their involvement with her. Indeed, Shakespeare has done, in a refractory way, what he saw Chaucer had
done before him, involve the onlooker's emotions with his heroine. I can think of no literary characters who have been subjected
to criticism less cool-headed than Criseyde and Cressida; and
when they are treated together they tend to become the two
halves of a companion picture, in which the good qualities of
the one are exactly balanced by the bad qualities of the other.
Criseyde is written up at Cressida's expense, and Cressida is
written down to Criseyde's advantage.

It is—or should be—an axiom of literary criticism that when
a critic sets out to prove a given work no good, he always succeeds, at least to his own satisfaction. This is evidenced by Johnson's marvelous destruction of *Lycidas*. Other critics, however,
less biased initially, are accustomed to find in the work real virtues to which the hostile critic has prudently blinded himself.
The same principle applies to literary characters. I note that Ber-
nard Shaw, in all of whose plays there hardly appears an uninteresting woman, is reported to have considered Cressida
Shakespeare's first real woman—he found her enchanting.[25] It
seems to me that if one approaches Cressida with an unpreju-
diced spirit one may see in her attractive qualities that escape the
prejudices of her non-admirers. Perhaps chief among these is
her vitality—I imagine it is that that fascinated Shaw—to which
the hostility she arouses in moralistic critics is a kind of backhanded tribute. Yet her speaking role in the play is small: she
speaks only 152 times, and 128 of her speeches are of less than
twenty words, 93 of less than ten.[26] She has only about half a
dozen longish speeches in the whole play. Moreover, almost
thirty percent of her speeches are, or contain, questions—a per-
centage that I doubt is exceeded by any other considerable character in Shakespeare. The brevity of her comments, their quick

staccato quality, imparts vitality to her; and her questions establish her as someone unsure of herself, but alert and seeking answers.[27] Lacking Chaucer's narrator as a companion, she seems
more independent than Criseyde; and lacking his total control
of the perspective and his ability to manipulate what we see, she
cannot share her predecessor's glamorous mystery and her motives may not be so veiled in ambiguity.

Yet Cressida's character has a marked ambiguity, though it is
of a different sort from Criseyde's. The fact is that all young
people, and especially attractive young women with independent minds, possess all sorts of potentialities, of qualities that
may with equal probability develop into something moralists
will call good, or something they will call bad. Since our judgment of Cressida must depend on her words—as well as on how
an actor reads her part—Shakespeare assigns her a number of
ambiguous speeches, speeches with two possible interpretations. Thus the wit with which she tries to defend herself in a
world full of snares for beautiful young women often invites, if
it does not always require, a secondary bawdy interpretation.
Hostile critics, prejudiced by their knowledge of her ultimate
treachery, and perhaps put off by her irreverent flippancy, seem
at times to go to unusual lengths to establish the bawdy side of
Cressida's conversation and to make her appear unusually liber-
tine of tongue. Actually, since no one has invented a scatologo-
meter by which to measure amounts of Elizabethan indecency,
we cannot accurately compare Cressida with heroines of better
reputation, but she figures no more prominently in Eric Partridge's study of Shakespearean obscenity than many of her
more innocent sisters[28]—even if we assume that every remark
of dubious meaning she makes has a bit of bawdry hiding in it.

Since Cressida's tongue has done so much to impeach her reputation, I shall look at a few of her speeches that have been
deemed by editors and critics most damaging to her character.
The first occurs when Pandarus is singing Troilus's praises and
she is pretending indifference. "Do you know a man if you see
him?" Pandarus asks her. She replies, "Ay, if I ever saw him
before and knew him" (I.ii.63–65). It is possible that all she is
doing here is aping Pandarus' conditional sentence to give a con-

ditionally negative answer: she suggests that she does not necessarily know and trust a man on first sight, but may do so after
some acquaintance. Some editors, however, insist that she is
being bawdy, punning on "before" and "knew": "If I ever saw
him from the front (i.e., before) and had sexual intercourse with
(i.e., knew) him." [29] I must say I find this a bit frail (and it has
not been adopted by the play's two most recent editors); [30] and I
worry about what would happen if every time we spoke the
words "before" and "knew" we were in real danger of making
dirty puns. Of course the context must control, but here the
context does not demand puns.

A little later Pandarus, in extravagant praise of Troilus, lists
all his wonderful qualities and asks if they are not "the spice and
salt that season a man." To this Cressida replies, "Ay, a minc'd
man; and then to be bak'd with no date in the pie, for then the
man's date is out" (I.ii.256–57). Cressida has picked up Pandarus's "salt and spice" and turned it into a full-fledged cooking
metaphor: any man with so many virtues must be a minced
meat-pie, which was usually cooked with dates, but omitted in
Troilus' case because he is out of date, presumably with Cressida. I cannot say that I find this very witty, but it is surely not
hard to understand with a little help from cookery. But the editor of the old Arden text, Deighton, appends the note, "it were
to consider too curiously to subject Cressida's meaning to a
strict scrutiny. Aristophanes would be the best scholiast here." [31]
Subsequent editors generally seem less ready to thrust bawdiness upon Cressida here, though editorial expectation of the
worst from her still leads to occasional bursts of philological
ingenuity. [32]

There are other examples of editors' blushing at Cressida so
busily that they neglect to tell us what they're blushing at. But
one undoubtedly bawdy passage, near the beginning of the play,
has, I think, more than any other been responsible for Cressida's
reputation for vulgarity. Pandarus acknowledges her minced-
man speech by saying, "You are such a woman, a man knows
not at what ward you lie." Cressida picks up the fencing imagery of "to lie at a ward," to take a position of defense, and
plays on it and puns on it in what for her is a long speech:

Upon my back, to defend my belly, upon my wit, to defend my wiles, upon my secrecy, to defend mine honesty, my mask, to defend my beauty, and you, to defend all these; and at all these wards I lie, at a thousand watches. [I.ii.258–64]

The annotator of the play in *The Riverside Shakespeare* asks the reader to "note the revealing language of physical conflict with which Cressida . . . describes her attitude toward men," and she surely does regard them as sexual aggressors. Furthermore, a woman who lies on her back to defend her belly seems to be offering herself up to sexual attack. But despite the immediate impression that the speech makes as one spoken by a woman who either is or wishes to be thought a thoroughly promiscuous wanton, its logic demands more attention than most editors since Samuel Johnson have been willing to give it.[33] It is obvious that Cressida does not rely on Pandarus, whom she knows to be a pimp, to defend her against men, any more than she would really lie on her back to defend her belly. Furthermore, wiles, which are refinements of wit, should not need the defense of wit; secrecy is not a true defense of honor (though I can't help noting that Chaucer's Criseyde is convinced that it is); and, finally, a mask that defends beauty from the sun also eliminates beauty by hiding it from view. Everything Cressida says seems to be either backward or askew. I think the speech is the ironically wry statement of one who realizes how inadequate her defenses are against Pandarus and Troilus from the outside and against her love for Troilus on the inside. She states her fears backward, as it were, punning when she says that she lies at all these wards.

And an even more real fear emerges as the conversation continues its bawdy way. Pandarus asks her to name one of her thousand watches, and she replies, "Nay, I'll watch you for that; and that's one of the chiefest of them," which I take to mean, No, I won't tell you any secrets because you're one of the principal things I have to watch out for. She continues: "If I cannot ward what I would not have hit, I can watch you for telling how I took the blow—unless it swell past hiding, and then it's past watching" (I.ii.266–70). To paraphrase: if I cannot defend my

chastity as I'd like to, I can expect you to tell how I lost it; unless
I get pregnant, in which case it's too late for defenses. Now that
this is all very shocking I cannot deny; and I may seem to com-
pound Cressida's offense by pointing out that she is one of the
only two ladies in Shakespeare's plays who use the indelicate
word *belly*. Yet the other is Celia, who when Rosalind implores
her to take the cork out of her mouth and reveal the identity of
the man who fastens verses to Rosalind on trees, replies, "So
you may put a man in your belly."[34] Actually, Celia is even more
vulgar than Cressida, whose use of the word is functional, emphasizing her very real fear of what a love affair may entail. I
remarked earlier that all a Trojan girl seems able to expect is a
lover, and when we meet Troilus, we are at once made aware
that he is not a lover who would heed Hermia's request to Lysander to "lie further off" (II.ii.43, 57). Here the difference between Cressida and Criseyde is very real, and not entirely to
Cressida's discredit. Chaucer's heroine was a heroine of medieval romance, and, for reasons unknown to gynecologists, un-
married heroines of medieval romance do not become pregnant
unless the plot they are involved in absolutely demands it. But
Cressida, living in the dying years of the Siege of Troy and of
the reign of Elizabeth I of England, had no such immunity.
Contemporary drama is full of problems involving girls who
did not get to the church in time. It seems to me that the passage
I have just analyzed is not just an exercise in free wit, idle and
spoken to establish Cressida as a tart, but is the complex expression of a very real and fully justified fear.[35] She is talking
obliquely to an issue, the issue presented by her love for Troilus,
whom Pandarus and her own heart are pressing upon her. She
is afraid of what might happen to her, including the likelihood
of pregnancy.

And the fact is that at this time, despite the impression the
passage may make, Cressida is not ready to surrender herself to
Troilus. At the end of the scene, having dismissed her uncle as a
"bawd," she delivers a soliloquy that has nothing bawdy about
it but has brought her as much opprobrium as her witty retorts.
She remarks on Pandarus' praise of Troilus, and then continues:

But more in Troilus thousandfold I see
Than in the glass of Pandar's praise may be;
Yet hold I off. Women are angels, wooing:
Things won are done, joy's soul lies in the doing.
That she belov'd knows nought that knows not this:
Men prize the thing ungain'd more than it is.
That she was never yet that ever knew
Love got so sweet as when desire did sue.
Therefore this maxim out of love I teach:
Achievement is command; ungain'd, beseech;
Then though my heart's content firm love doth bear,
Nothing of that shall from mine eyes appear.   [I.ii.284–95]

According to one critic, this soliloquy proclaims Cressida's "simple creed, the art of the coquette raised to a Rule of Life, based on the assumption that what is to be looked for in Man is simply 'lust in action.'"[36] Yet the rhyming couplets could be taken as memorized advice from her mother, recited by a girl of no experience—straightforward self-preservative advice based on the not wholly misguided assumption (in Troy, at least) that what is to be found in man is lust in action. In his matching soliloquy, just before the lovers meet, Troilus looks forward to an opportunity to "wallow in the lily-beds /Propos'd for the deserver" of Cressida's favors (III.ii.12–13)—a not unlustful program of action. Cressida's maxims are, like most maxims, ungenerous but sensibly prudent; they were recognized as maxims by the printer of the Quarto of the play, who surrounded three of them with the quotation marks accorded to gnomic sayings in Elizabethan play texts.[37] But of course if one has decided that Cressida is a slut, then flirtatiousness, which may appear as the incidental by-product of prudent holding off, is all she is given credit for. Chaucer's Criseyde held off far longer and for far less apparent reason, and no one has ever chided her for it.

But Cressida fails to hold off from Troilus—and I have not noticed that any of those who condemn the self-centeredness of her holding off congratulate her for the generosity of her surrender, apparently taking it as further proof of her sluttishness. Such critics are apt to suppose it to be coyness when, just before

she meets Troilus, Pandarus describes her as blushing and fetch-
ing "her wind so short, as if she were fray'd with a spirit"
(III.ii.32), but it is hard to see why she is not simply frightened
at what she is about to do.[38] Her embarrassed speech to Troilus,
in which she tries to explain to him why she was so hard to win,
is sometimes called insincere, though the text lacks any evidence
of insincerity.[39] It is said also that when she says to Troilus,
"Stop my mouth" (133), because she is afraid she is professing
her love for him too unguardedly, she is really begging for the
kiss she denies she is begging for.[40] Considering that she and
Troilus have just completed a remarkably long kiss, if one mea-
sures it by the length of Pandarus's verbal accompaniment
(something Shakespeare borrowed from Chaucer), and that the
rest of the evening promises no dearth of kisses, her words seem
redundant as flirtation. Nor does her earlier speech, which even
her harshest critics grudgingly admit she thinks is sincere,[41] betray any of the speciousness of a flirt:

> Boldness comes to me now, and brings me heart.
> Prince Troilus, I have lov'd you night and day
> For many weary months.   [113–15]

These are the words of any good Shakespearean heroine con-
fessing her love with most engaging candor, and are the exact
emotional equivalent of Chaucer's Criseyde's answer when,
bedded at last, Troilus tells her she must yield:

> Ne had I er now, my swete hart dere,
> Been yold, iwis, I were now not here.   [III 1210–11]

In the play, after introducing the lovers, Pandarus goes to get
fire—a kind of altered echo of an incident in which Chaucer's
Pandarus removes the light and himself from the bed in which
Troilus and Criseyde are lying and goes to the fireplace. As soon
as her uncle has gone, Shakespeare's Cressida says to Troilus,
"Will you walk in, my lord?" (60), but Troilus continues to talk
to her. At the end of their conversation Cressida once more says,
"Will you walk in, my lord?" (99). Joyce Carol Oates calls these
invitations "a blunt undercutting of [Troilus'] poetry;"[42] but in
fact they are only imitations of her admired Chaucerian prede-

cessor, who, as we have seen, also had sometimes to interrupt her talkative lover. And Cressida has the excuse that she might wish to escape from her omnipresent uncle: one recalls that Criseyde's much nicer uncle spent the night in the same room as the lovers—at least there is nothing in the text to indicate that he didn't—a fate Cressida may be anxious to avoid. But Troilus' preoccupation with self-expression results in Pandarus' returning and remaining with them throughout their professions of love.

In stressing the potentiality for innocence in Cressida I am not denying the other side: I am merely trying to restore a more equal balance between the two faces of ambiguity. In the curious physics of literature, suspicion of absence of innocence always seems to have greater specific gravity than recognition of the possibility of its presence. Most Chaucerian critics have found merely charming Criseyde's reply to her uncle when, the morning after her first night with Troilus, he comes to her and asks her how she feels:

> neuer the bet for you,
> Foxe that ye been, God yeue your hart care:
> God helpe me so, ye caused all this fare.   [III 1564–66]

But Shakespearean critics find gross Cressida's remark to Pandarus when he returns and finds them still conversing: "Well, uncle, what folly I commit, I dedicate to you" (102–03). To me, these speeches seem very similar if one allows for Cressida's greater directness and her less than large respect for her uncle. But this is perhaps prejudice.

I cannot, however, deny that it is sometimes difficult not to put the worst construction on Cressida's words, and to assign her a less than creditable meaning, even where the possibility of a more decent meaning persists. When she says to her lover, all too hurriedly departing from her at dawn,

> Prithee, tarry,
> You men will never tarry.
> O foolish Cressid! I might have still held off,
> And then you would have tarried,   [IV.ii. 15–18]

she may only be voicing, wryly, the truth of the maxims she recited earlier and has ignored; or expressing the ancient female complaint that men ration their moments of tenderness too severely and end them too abruptly. But that the words could come naturally from a woman of experience in bed matters is undeniable. And even readers most anxious to see innocence in Cressida are not much supported by her lover. When, a little later, hearing knocking at the gate, Cressida says to Troilus, "My lord, come you again into my chamber," and then adds, after a pause, "You smile and mock me, as if I meant naughtily," his reply is a rude "Ha, ha!" (36–38). Her denial that she intended the pun on the word *chamber* that he heard is justifiably indignant: he's treating her as if she were a whore.

Arnold Stein remarks that Cressida "has a trick, which might have provided Freud with useful examples, of slyly provoking indecent jokes at which she can be embarrassed."[43] Stripped of its prejudice—"slyly" and "can be"—this is a just remark: Shakespeare does indeed present Cressida as one *fated* to provoke indecent jokes at which she *is* embarrassed. Indeed, the double entendres and potential double entendres that her witticisms so often are suggest that it is by a kind of extended use of double entendre that Shakespeare imparts to her much of her ambiguity. Shakespeare keeps giving us images, in microcosm, of her history. She is fated ultimately to show the world two different sides of her personality, a good one and a bad one, just as Criseyde had done in Chaucer's poem. It is her good side that many critics have willfully tried to conceal behind the bad one that finally triumphs. Criseyde also had the potentiality to show two sides, but Chaucer's sleight-of-hand managed to keep the bad one hidden behind the good one until the very last book. Yet the two Cressid-figures, though in many ways dissimilar, are in some important ways alike; and they have equally valid claim on our sympathy.

5

Lovers' Problems:
Troilus and Criseyde and
Troilus and Cressida

he exchange in Shakespeare's play between Troilus and Cressida in which he understands her to have made an indecent pun ("My lord, come you again into my chamber") that she denies having intended to make, though it is perhaps the supreme example of how Shakespeare uses double entendre to achieve Cressida's ambiguity, also tells us something unambiguous about her lover.

Chaucer's Troilus is an inexperienced idealist, capable of getting so lost in his own thoughts as to become paralyzed; but with Criseyde he is a thoughtful and considerate lover. He puts the maintenance of her "honor" first in his scale of values—even before his love for her—with the result that, when her exchange for Antenor is arranged between the Trojans and the Greeks, there is nothing Troilus can do to prevent her going to the Greek camp: any action he takes will reveal their relationship and thus ruin Criseyde's "honor,"[1] which depends, like Cressida's "honesty," on secrecy. Yet in the poem one feels that Pandarus may well have been right in suggesting to Troilus that if he did something forceful to keep her in Troy—kidnap her, for instance—she might soon forgive him.[2] Much in her character suggests that she needed and wanted someone who would do her really important decision making for her. In a way, she had earlier allowed Pandarus to do this, and though one hates to think of it, she was later to allow Diomede to do it.

And though the narrator, heaven knows, never mentions it, Troilus and Criseyde do seem to be something of a mismatch. Theirs is the common human situation in which one of the partners in a love affair possesses high ideals which the other admires—even loves—without sharing, and which may prove exasperating at times to one who feels that it is better to adjust to an unwanted reality than to uphold ideals at all costs. Troilus' very solicitude for Criseyde, though in all respects admirable, is in some respects a bit exasperating to the reader—and perhaps to Criseyde. Both Pandarus and Troilus independently think of the possibility of preventing Criseyde's exchange by kidnapping her, and surely Criseyde must have thought of it too. But though Troilus allows Pandarus to believe that he will raise the issue with her—will ask her permission[3]—Troilus fails to do so. Why he fails to do so we never learn, but one suspects that it is because he knows in his heart that she would say no, as her outwardly conventional and publicly decorous nature would dictate her doing. Troilus' failure to take a strong position is emphasized when, instead of asking her permission to kidnap her, he suggests that they steal away from Troy altogether;[4] this is an ignominious solution that she naturally refuses.

A lover less thoughtful might well have taken the matter into his own hands without asking her, as Pandarus originally suggested. But to make Criseyde a party to the decision—no, that will never do. One recalls in *Antony and Cleopatra* how Menas asked Pompey's permission to eliminate the Second Triumvirate by putting out to sea with its members; Pompey replies, "Ah, this thou shouldst have done, / And not have spoke on't! . . . Thou must know, / 'Tis not my profit that does lead mine honor; / Mine honor, it" (II.vii.73–77). Like Menas, Troilus might have been forgiven—even been congratulated—if he'd acted without asking, but his sacred regard for Criseyde's honor prevents any practical action. Yet Criseyde herself admits, once she is in the Greek camp, that it would have been wiser for her to pursue her own profit with Troilus than to preserve her honor.[5]

Shakespeare noticed the mismatch of Troilus and Criseyde and imitated it while altering its nature. He awarded his Cres-

sida a much less sensitive and suitable lover than Chaucer's Troilus.[6] Shakespeare's Troilus has his forerunner's ability to get lost
in his own head, so lost, indeed, that he hardly seems aware that
Cressida is a person as well as a mistress. The sensuous soliloquy
in which he looks forward to a chance to "wallow in the lily-
beds" she has to offer manages to omit her entirely[7] (aside from
the flower-bed imagery): it's all about Troilus (III.ii.8–29). He
is, of course, capable of marvelous poetry—which has made
him a favorite with some critics[8]—but it's generally spoken to
as well as about himself. When he first meets Cressida, he exclaims, "You have bereft me of all words, lady" (ii.54), but the
fact is that he has, as the falling end of this line suggests, been
bereft of iambic pentameter: the only prose he speaks in the entire play is to Cressida on their first meeting. It is Cressida who
gets them back into the verse we should expect of Shakespearean lovers meeting for the first time. The change to verse
occurs in her highly embarrassed but very moving profession of
her love for Troilus (113–51); this profession is so filled with her
sense of her own inadequacy that at one point she tries to leave
the stage, offended, as she says, by her own company. She
simply cannot keep straight the various issues urgent in her
mind: her overpowering love, the fears that had caused her pre-
tended coldness, and her consciousness—and here Shakespeare
makes her aware of her own ambiguity—that what she is saying
stumblingly in all sincerity could be construed as specious flirtation:

> Perchance, my lord, I show more craft than love,
> And fell so roundly to a large confession,
> To angle for your thoughts.

Her confusion is very apparent in the marvelous non-sequitur[9]
with which she finishes this admission:

> but you are wise,
> Or else you love not; for to be wise and love
> Exceeds man's might; that dwells with gods above.   [153–57]

The ancient cliché, that love and wisdom are incompatible, may
not by any wrenching of sense be made into a proof of the prop-

osition that Troilus is either wise or else does not love her. In her confusion, Cressida draws a conclusion opposite to the one her proposition calls for, forcing ambiguity upon clarity.

Actually, in the entire scene in which the lovers first meet, Troilus never does speak a speech of lyric love, in prose or poetry; the profession is all Cressida's to him, not his to her. And, skipping ahead for a moment, I note that Troilus' alba in the morning is one of the briefest and most reluctant ever spoken. It gets off to a good start: "Are you aweary of me?" Cressida asks him, and he replies,

> O Cressida! but that the busy day,
> Wak'd by the lark, hath rous'd the ribald crows,
> And dreaming night will hide our joys no longer,
> I would not from thee. [IV.ii.8–11]

Here his poetic power seems to flag, and Cressida has to lend him a helping hand, which she does with the terse statement of his theme: "Night hath been too brief." Troilus starts up again with some enthusiasm:

> Beshrew the witch! with venomous wights she stays
> As tediously as hell, but flies the grasps of love
> With wings more momentary-swift than thought.
> You will catch cold and curse me. [12–15]

Never did Pegasus take a worse tumble than in this ill-timed worry about Cressida's health—something we might have expected of the solicitous Chaucerian Troilus, except that he was too sensible a lover to have volunteered it at such a moment. Cressida's next speech is one I discussed in the last chapter, her complaint that men will never tarry. I am not sure that Troilus' aborted alba does not offer a very good excuse for her petulance.

But to return to the scene of their first meeting: Cressida's confused but still eloquent profession of love does not, as I said, draw a reciprocal profession from Troilus. It does, however, enable him to start talking on what is to become his favorite subject, which is his own high potential for maintaining constancy in love. He characteristically introduces his speech by implying that Cressida's potential for constancy is dubious:

> O that I thought it could be in a woman—
> As, if it can, I will presume in you—
> To feed for aye her lamp and flames of love,
> To keep her constancy in plight and youth,
> Outliving beauties outward, with a mind
> That doth renew swifter than blood decays!   [III.ii.158–63]

"O that I thought" introduces a wish contrary-to-fact: Troilus does not think it possible for a woman to keep her constancy in plight and youth; if, however, this unlikely situation should occur, Troilus, with belated courtesy tucked away in the apodosis of a conditional sentence, will presume it to exist in Cressida. But he does not now think it could occur—he needs persuasion:

> Or that persuasion could but thus convince me
> That my integrity and truth to you
> Might be affronted with the match and weight
> Of such a winnowed purity in love!
> How were I then uplifted!   [164–68]

If persuasion could (rather tautologically) persuade him that Cressida could offer him the winnowed purity in love which he is capable of, how much he would be uplifted. "But alas!" he continues, using the adversative conjunction to introduce what the OED would call "a statement of the nature of an exception, objection, limitation, or contrast to what has gone before"[10]— that is, the possibility of Cressida's constancy:

> but alas,
> I am as true as truth's simplicity,
> And simpler than the infancy of truth.   [168–70]

His very syntax excludes the possibility that that is something Cressida could ever be.

The fact that Troilus turns out to be right in his discourteous suggestion that Cressida will not prove true should not blind us to the fact that he has no right to be right. He is, indeed, seeing in the fountain of their love dregs more obtrusive than Cressida had earlier said she saw, but had left undefined.[11] Furthermore, Troilus has started to refer to a love match as if it were a boxing match, emphasizing not union but competition. Cressida is sen-

sitive to the implications of rivalry and replies in kind: "In that
[constancy] I'll war with you." This brings the exclamation, "O
virtuous fight" from a Troilus now happy that Cressida has accepted her role as an antagonist, "When right with right wars
who shall be most right!"

In Chaucer, Criseyde's acknowledgment of the role she will
come to play in literary history does not occur until after she has
decided to accept Diomede as her lover in place of Troilus. In a
monologue addressed both to the absent Troilus and to the future readership of the poem, she laments her sad, fated treachery:

> Alas, for now is clene ago
> My name in trouth of loue for euermo,
> For I haue falsed one the gentillest
> That euer was, and one the worthiest.
>
> Alas, of me vnto the worlds end
> Shal neither been ywritten or ysong
> No good word, for these bokes wol me shend.
> Irolled shal I been on many a tong;
> Throughout the world my bel shal be rong.
> And women most wol hate me of all—
> Alas that soch a caas me should fall.   [V 1054–64]

Since within the poem Criseyde's falseness is known surely only
to Pandarus and Troilus, who have no reason to speak of it publicly, it seems that Criseyde has been reading her own story in
other books—in Benoît or Boccaccio. In Shakespeare's play,
Troilus, Cressida, and Pandarus are also already familiar with
the story, with the result that Cressida is forced to foreshadow
her infidelity even before she sleeps with Troilus, and it is he
who forces her to do so. He completes his speech about right
warring with right as follows:

> True swains in love shall in the world to come,
> Approve their truth by Troilus. When their rhymes,
> Full of protest, of oath and big compare,
> Wants similes, truth tir'd with iteration,
> As true as steel, as plantage to the moon,
> As sun to day, as turtle to her mate,
> As iron to adamant, as earth to th'centre

Yet after all comparisons of truth
(As truth's authentic author to be cited)
"As true as Troilus" shall crown up the verse,
And sanctify the numbers. [173–83]

Chaucer's Troilus is indeed also true in love, but nowhere does Chaucer convert him into a byword for truth. Shakespeare's Troilus has been reading Henryson as well as Chaucer, for Henryson is the first considerable poet to celebrate Troilus' truth and to counterbalance it rhetorically with Cressida's falseness. It is Henryson's Cresseid who makes the contrast in her fine lament after she has become a begging leper and has been given largesse by her revivified former lover (who does not recognize her). The first line of her lament is, "O false Creseide, and true knight Troilus," and this is repeated several times as a kind of refrain in her lament.[12] Shakespeare's Cressida also seems to know her Henryson as well as her Chaucer, for, forced by Troilus' rhetoric, which has preempted truth, she accepts the need to express her own potentiality for constancy largely in terms of falseness. At the end of Troilus' boast of his truth she exclaims, with sad irony, "Prophet may you be!" and then continues with an eloquence that perhaps gives her a slight edge in this war of opposite words:

If I be false, or swerve a hair from truth,
When time is old, and hath forgot itself,
When water-drops have worn the stones of Troy,
And blind oblivion swallow'd cities up,
And mighty states characterless are grated
To dusty nothing, yet let memory,
From false to false among false maids in love,
Upbraid my falsehood! When th' have said as false
As air, as water, wind, or sandy earth,
As fox to lamb, as wolf to heifer's calf,
Pard to the hind, or step-dame to her son,
Yea, let them say, to stick the heart of falsehood,
"As false as Cressid." [184–96]

The poor little one-line protasis beginning "If I be false" is swallowed up in a monstrous twelve-line apodosis describing a world from which all is gone but falsehood, and leading up to the climax, "As false as Cressid." The "if" of the protasis simply disappears, and the conditional apodoses take on the effect of future indicatives: "as false as Cressid" *will* become a byword.

Pandarus now enters the competition, as ever speaking prose, and, like Cressida, with a conditional sentence:

> Go to, a bargain made, seal it, seal it. I'll be the witness. Here I hold your hand, here my cousin's. If ever you prove false one to another, since I have taken such pains to bring you together, let all pitiful goers-between be call'd to the world's end after my name; call them all Pandars. Let all constant men be Troiluses, all false women Cressids, and all brokers between Pandars!
>
> [197–204]

Like the lovers, he's been reading the old story too, as his faulty logic shows: good sense would otherwise require that after the protasis that posits the possibility of either lover being unfaithful to the other Pandarus should say, "Let all *in*constant men be Troiluses," in order to match calling all false women Cressids. The text has sometimes been emended to this reading;[13] but the sentence as it stands accurately prophesies the literary tradition that Troilus and Cressida are in the process of reenacting.

Pandarus' proposition that if the lovers he has brought together are false to one another his name will become a word for pimp seems to have its roots in Chaucer, though Shakespeare—as always in his treatment of Pandarus—is making coarsely explicit something that is at most implicit in Chaucer. Chaucer's Pandarus shows himself aware, in one of his conversations with Troilus just before the consummation scene, that the service he is performing for Troilus is in fact that of a pimp. Troilus indignantly denies that it is any such thing, on the rather fragile ground that a pimp only becomes a pimp by taking money for his servies: it is clear that Pandarus is acting through friendship and not for profit (III 238–420). Nevertheless, the exact nature of Pandarus' services is a disturbing question that lies just beneath the surface of the narrative. The narrator, of course, describes Pandarus' services to the lovers with enthusiastic approbation, but in precisely the terms one would use if one were simply describing the actions of an efficient pimp—as, for instance, in the following lines that refer to the interval between the scene at Deiphobus' house and the dinner at Pandarus': Pandarus

> . . . shoue aie on, he to and fro was sent,
> He letters bare when Troilus was absent—   [III 487–88]

a genuine go-between performing "messagerye," in the sense that it is used in the allegorical description of the garden of the Temple of Priapus in *The Parliament of Fowls* (228).

And, of course, at the end of the poem, when Pandarus is finally forced to admit what in his heart he has long known, that Criseyde has become unfaithful, he refers guardedly to the true nature of the service he had performed "at Troilus' request":

> And that thou me besoughtest don of yore,
> Hauing vnto mine honour ne my rest
> Right no regard, I did all that the lest.   [V 1734–36]

He forgets that he offered his services before Troilus asked for them, having himself no regard for his honor nor his peace of mind. Criseyde's behavior has now made him hate her (V 1732)—most sadly, for he had loved her in his way—and one feels that his hatred comes from his realization of the truth of the proposition that Shakespeare's Pandarus was to lay down: since one of the lovers has proved false to the other, Pandarus, who brought them together, must now be known as a pimp. The transformation of his proper name to an occupational name took place in English as a result of his part in Chaucer's poem— despite the narrator's refusal to recognize him for what he is— so that in Shakespeare's play he already is what he predicts he may become.

But to return to the lovers. Troilus and Cressida assent to Pandarus' proposition by joining in his "Amen"; he dispatches them to bed, and then, unlike his Chaucerian predecessor, intrudes on them no more until morning.[14] He reappears shortly after Cressida's complaint about men's never tarrying, and, as Cressida has foreseen that he will, he teases her about her night of love. This is a rather unsavory scene that I may not pass over in silence:

Pandarus. How now, how now, how go maidenheads?
  Here, you maid! where's my cousin Cressid?
Cressida. Go hang yourself, you naughty mocking uncle!
  You bring me to do—and then you flout me too.
Pandarus. To do what, to do what? let her say what. What
  have I brought you to do?
Cressida. Come, come, beshrew your heart, you'll ne'er be
  good, nor suffer others.
Pandarus. Ha, ha! Alas, poor wretch! A poor capocchia! hast
  not slept tonight? Would he not, a naughty man, let it sleep?
  A bugbear take him!
Cressida. Did I not tell you? Would he were knock'd i'th'head!
                                                    [IV.ii.23–34]

Distasteful as one may find this exchange, it has its firm roots in
Chaucer. In talking in the last chapter about Cressida's dedication to her uncle of the folly she commits, I mentioned Chaucer's Pandarus' visit to Criseyde as she lay in bed after Troilus
had left her in the morning after their first night together. I shall
give the whole passage:

Pandare, a morowe which that comen was
Unto his nece and gan her faire grete,
And saied, "All this night so rained it, alas,
That all my drede is that ye, nece swete,
Haue little leiser had to slepe and mete.
All this night," quod he, "hath rain so do me wake,
That some of vs, I trowe, her heddes ake."

And nere he came & said, "How stant it now
This merie morow? Nece, how can ye fare?"
Creseide answerd, "Neuer the bet for you,
Foxe that ye been—God yeue your hart care!
God helpe me so, ye caused all this fare!
Trowe I," quod she, "for all your words white,
O, who so seeth you knoweth you full lite."

With that she gan her face for to wrie
With the shete, and woxe for shame all redde.
And Pandarus gan vnder for to prie,
And saied, "Nece, if that I shall been dedde,
Haue here a sworde and smiteth off my hedde."

With that his arme all sodainly he thrist
Under her necke and at the last her kist. [III 1555–75]

Now one makes what one wants of this scene, so charmingly playful, and with such potentially sinister undertones. As I have said elsewhere,[15] critics forty years ago used to mention its charm and skate very quickly over its meaning as over thin ice, whereas nowadays critics are apt to fall into it and drown in its Freudian depths. Chaucer encourages our suspicions with a brilliantly ambiguous comment:

I passe all that which chargeth naught to say:
What, God foryaue his death, and she also
Foryaue, and with her vncle gan to plaie,
For other cause was ther none than so.
But of this thing right to theffect to go,
Whan time was, home to her house she went,
And Pandarus hath fully his entent. [1576–82]

Tasteless as it is, Shakespeare's version of this morning-after encounter not only fails to exploit the more horrid latencies present in Chaucer but also suppresses the worst of them entirely. I shudder to think what Thersites would have made of the old poet's scene. In any case, we should not in this instance hold anything more against Cressida and her uncle than against Criseyde and her uncle.

In the play, when at the knocking at the gate, Cressida invites Troilus back into her chamber, with the result that Troilus—not Pandarus, who is present and of whom we might have expected it—laughs at what he takes to be her indecent pun, she replies, "Come, you are deceived, I think of no such thing" (39). As the knocking persists, Cressida repeats her invitation, saying she "would not for half Troy" have him seen in her house. Cressida's critical enemies say that she is here thinking about her own honor rather than Troilus', and they may be right. But if she is, she is only following in the footsteps of her esteemed Chaucerian predecessor,[16] though she receives less cooperation from her lover. Aeneas bursts in asking for Troilus, and Troilus, who has briefly withdrawn with Cressida, promptly reappears, impervious to any worry about Cressida's reputation. Even Uncle

Pandarus makes a feeble effort to conceal Troilus' presence in the house from Aeneas (51–53). After Troilus hears from Aeneas that an exchange of Cressida for Antenor has been arranged and is to be executed forthwith, Troilus does ask Aeneas not to tell anyone he has been there, but the request is a casual one, seeming like an afterthought. The self-possession with which Troilus takes Aeneas' bad news is remarkable. He first asks, "Is it so concluded?" and on learning that it is, he exclaims "How my achievements mock me!" (66, 69). Cressida's prudential soliloquy has been proved right: "Achievement is command," and since she has become one of Troilus' achievements, he will soon be commanding her to go to the Greek camp.

When Troilus and Aeneas have left, Pandarus, with a show of reluctance, tells Cressida of the exchange. Characteristically, he sets a precedent for critics by worrying about the effect of the separation on Troilus rather than on Cressida (85–86), whom he blames for being the cause of so much unhappiness to Troilus. Cressida's first reaction to the news is to exclaim, "O you immortal gods! I will not go!" and to Pandarus' terse reply, "Thou must," she says, "I will not, uncle" (94–96). Then, after denying—as her forebear had[17]—that the blood relationship to her father had any weight compared to her love for Troilus, she continues:

> O you gods divine,
> Make Cressid's name the very crown of falsehood,
> If ever she leave Troilus! [99–101]

This is another of Shakespeare's perverse echoes of Chaucer. When Pandarus is discussing with Chaucer's Troilus Criseyde's impending exchange and urging him to do something to prevent it, he gives him a sinister warning:

> And if she wilneth fro thee for to passe,
> Than is she false, so loue her wel the lasse. [IV 615–16]

It would be unfair to say that Chaucer's Criseyde "wilneth" (wants) to go to the Greek camp, but her resignation to her having to go is almost as quick and absolute as the determination of Shakespeare's Cressida not to go. The ironic prophecy

implicit in Pandarus' warning Shakespeare transfers to Cressida
herself and expresses negatively: Chaucer's Pandarus suggests
that her willingness to leave Troilus is itself a proof of Criseyde's
infidelity; Cressida, on the other hand, asks that her name become the "crown of falsehood" if she ever does leave him.

I mentioned earlier the overwriting that Chaucer's narrator is
guilty of in the depiction of Criseyde's extravagant grief at the
prospect of having to leave Troy—how theatrically she tore her
"ounded" hair that was "sunnish" of hue, and let its "mighty
tresses" hang all unbraided about her ears.[18] The slightly specious impression that this overwriting produces is totally absent
from the grief that Shakespeare's Cressida expresses. With a
slight bow to Chaucer's narrator, however, Shakespeare has
Cressida vow to

> Tear my bright hair, and scratch my praised cheeks,
> Crack my clear voice with sobs, and break my heart,
> With sounding Troilus. I will not go from Troy.   [106–08]

In threatening to imitate her predecessor's behavior she seems
momentarily to be tearing Criseyde's bright hair.[19] But in the
conclusion of her speech, insisting that she will not go from
Troy, she is most unlike her predecessor.

Unfortunately her lover, unlike her predecessor's lover, re-
signs himself—and her—to her going as immediately as ever
did Criseyde in Chaucer.[20] When Troilus returns to find Cressida in tears, he addresses her in words that at once deny any
possibility of her remaining in the city:

> Cressid, I love thee in so strain'd a purity
> That the blest gods, as angry with my fancy,
> More bright in zeal than the devotion which
> Cold lips blow to their deities, take thee from me. [IV.iv.24–27]

From the Troilus who earlier had asked the Trojan council,
"What's aught but as 'tis valued?" (II.ii.52) and argued against
restoring Helen to the Greeks, we might expect a reaction less
submissive to a mere decree that is taking from him what he
purports to value most. Nothing earlier in the play and nothing
later suggests that Troilus had any special reverence for the

gods, whose power—and malignancy—he sees at work behind
the decree. "Have the gods envy?" Cressida asks, and he replies,
"Ay, ay, ay, ay, 'tis too plain a case."

> *Cressida*. And is it true that I must go from Troy?
> *Troilus*. A hateful truth.
> *Cressida*.   What, and from Troilus too?
> *Troilus*. From Troy and Troilus.
> *Cressida*.   Is't possible?
> *Troilus*. And suddenly. . . .   [IV.iv.29–33]

He then launches into a splendid speech about their enforced
hasty farewell—"Injurious time now with a robber's haste /
Crams his rich thiev'ry up"—which is interrupted by a call
from Aeneas within, "My lord, is the lady ready?" Says Troilus,

> Hark, you are call'd. Some say the Genius so
> Cries "come" to him that instantly must die.
> —Bid them have patience, she shall come anon.   [50–52]

Cressida, not, perhaps, hearing the voice of Genius crying to
her before her instant death, asks, "I must then to the Grecians?"
Troilus's reply is a brief, "No remedy," and though he may think
this true, a more considerate lover would have explained more
fully why there is no remedy. Rebuffed by his answer, Cressida
exclaims, "A woeful Cressid 'mongst the merry Greeks! When
shall we see again?" Troilus begins his reply, "Hear me, love. Be
thou but true of heart—" when Cressida interrupts in surprise:
"I true? How now? what wicked deem is this?" Troilus' aborted
speech can be taken, as perhaps Cressida takes it, as the protasis
of a conditional sentence: If only you are true; this would not be
the first time that Troilus has shown himself willing to allow for
a woman's being faithful only in the conditional mood. To Cressida's interruption he gives a most curious reply:

> Nay, we must use expostulation kindly,
> For it is parting from us.
> I speak not "be thou true" as fearing thee,
> For I will throw my glove to Death himself
> That there is no maculation in thy heart;

But "be thou true" say I to fashion in
My sequent protestation: be thou true,
And I will see thee.   [60–67]

I must say that I can follow his logic only with great difficulty.
He abandons the conditional, which he seems to be explaining
away as a mere rhetorical convenience, and restates the idea so
as still to make their seeing one another the consequence of her
being true: "be thou true" is now clearly an imperative—be true
and I will come. This is still not very lover-like. It is, of course,
finely ironical that when he does next see Cressida, she is being
false, though this hardly excuses his rude if prophetic wisdom.
Cressida seems satisfied with the answer, however, and exclaims
at the dangers he will face if he comes to the Greek camp, adding, to reassure him, "but I'll be true."

The lovers exchange gifts, and Cressida asks again when she
will see Troilus. He promises "nightly visitation," and then
adds, obsessively, "But yet be true" (74). An exasperated Cressida, quite justly feeling that Troilus is not using expostulation
very kindly (she might have wondered why their farewell
speeches should have been labeled expostulation in the first
place), exclaims, "O heavens! 'Be true' again?" In a speech derived from Chaucer's Troilus, her lover then explains that the
Greeks are such highly accomplished wooers of women that he
is afraid Cressida may be "moved" by their personal charms and
their "novelty" (75–82). Chaucer's Criseyde, on hearing similar
distrustful words from her lover after vowing eternal fidelity to
him, had said, You don't trust me (IV 1606–10). Shakespeare's
Cressida, even more justifiably indignant because she had man-
ifested only complete unwillingness to go to the Greek camp
where she would meet these practiced wooers, cries, "O heavens! You love me not." Troilus's reply is a masterly example of
the kind of tact that fails to repair a breach of tact. "Die I a villain
then!" he exclaims: "In this I do not call your faith in question /
So mainly as my merit." The second clause is intended to reinforce the meaning of the first, but actually it tends to cancel it:
he *is* calling her faith into question, though not as much as his
own deserts. He then reverts to the charms of the Greeks in
whom

There lurks a still and dumb-discoursive devil
That tempts most cunningly, but be not tempted.   [90–91]

"Do you think I will?" Cressida asks. "No," he replies, "but"—
and the adversative conjunction introduces a speech of large
wisdom and little tact:

But something may be done that we will not,
And sometimes we are devils to ourselves,
When we will tempt the frailty of our powers,
Presuming on their changeful potency.

Troilus has now successfully maneuvered himself into the position of one addressing a woman who is stubbornly determined
to go to the Greek camp to test her constancy against the better
judgment of himself, who would strongly advise her not to go:
he has, indeed, succeeded in changing places psychologically
with his Chaucerian predecessor, despite the fact that he has not
even considered the possibility of his mistress' not going, and
that, unlike her predecessor, she is desperately eager that he stop
her going. At this point it seems that Chaucer's Troilus, who
tries at least weakly to stop Criseyde from going, would have
been a better match for Shakespeare's Cressida, who doesn't
want to go, and Chaucer's Criseyde, who is willing to go, a
more appropriate one for Shakespeare's Troilus, who has made
no effort to prevent her going.

A call from Paris and Aeneas within cuts off any reply by
Cressida to Troilus' last bit of expostulation. Troilus bids her,
"Come kiss, and let us part," and her last words to him are, "My
lord, will you be true?"—a perhaps needless but still very natural question. It elicits from Troilus one last boast about his fidelity:

Who, I? Alas, it is my vice, my fault:
Whiles others fish with craft for great opinion,
I with great truth catch mere simplicity;
Whilst some with cunning gild their copper crowns,
With truth and plainness I do wear mine bare.
Fear not my truth: the moral of my wit
Is "plain and true"; that's all the reach of it.   [102–08]

Well, I suppose Cressida brought it on herself. But it almost seems by the time she is led away by Diomed, that Troilus is welcoming the separation—even Cressida's possible infidelity—as providing the most favorable circumstances in which to exhibit his fidelity. The egotism implicit in any great idealism was in the case of Chaucer's Troilus counterbalanced by his genuine concern for Criseyde's well-being, but the devotion to truth of Shakespeare's Troilus seems a quality that excludes everyone but himself: it is a fault, a vice, in a way other than the one he thinks it. I have sometimes felt that Cressida's decision to take up with Diomed is more understandable than was Criseyde's, who abandoned her lover before he could abandon her—as he never did. Yet her Troilus went on loving her even after he fully realized her infidelity, whereas the later Troilus' love turns to bitter hatred that makes him a madman on the battlefield.

But of course Cressida remains an unforgivable heroine of a love story. She fulfills her responsibility to literary history and becomes a daughter of the game, thus making an honest prophet out of Ulysses. But up until the very end her role in the play retains its ambiguity; even her penultimate scene with the Greek generals is ambiguous: it is in this that she presumably performs the actions for which Ulysses finds grounds for condemning her in the speech with the first lines of which I began the last chapter. Cressida and Diomed enter into the view of the Greek generals, and Agamemnon, spying the pair, asks, "Is not yond Diomed, with Calchas' daughter?" Ulysses' answer should caution us against mistaking him for a very accurate judge of people's characters from the way they move:[21]

> 'Tis he. I ken the manner of his gait,
> He rises on the toe. That spirit of his
> In aspiration lifts him from the earth.   [IV.v.14–16]

Anyone who can see from the way Diomed walks his spirit lifting him from the earth in aspiration should have his vision checked by a psycho-oculist: never was there a crasser, more cynical, flatly realistic womanizer than Diomed, whose aspiration will lift him knee-high, to Cressida's bed.

Cressida, upon entering to the generals, is greeted by Aga-

memnon with a polite speech of welcome and a kiss, which I
take to be his privilege as commander-in-chief of the Greek
forces. Nestor then diplomatically informs her who it is who
has just kissed her: "Our general doth salute you with a kiss"
(19). It is here that Ulysses, apparently already hearing the silent
Cressida's foot speak and noting the wanton spirits looking out
at every joint and motive of her body, makes his witty suggestion:

> Yet is the kindness but particular,
> 'Twere better she were kiss'd in general—   [20–21]

a nice use of the passive voice to establish Cressida's status as an
object to be acted upon by the Greek brass. Nestor then begins
the kissing game, followed by Achilles, followed by Patroclus,
who kisses her twice, once for himself and once for Menelaus
the cuckold. Cressida is thus kissed five times without speaking
a word: presumably by this point in the play she is used to being
treated as if she had no feelings worth anyone's consulting. It is
not until Menelaus insists upon having his own kiss that she
speaks—wittily, offensively in both senses of the word, but de-
fensively too. Indeed, the text indicates that she succeeds in
avoiding having to be kissed by Menelaus. Ulysses, the next
officer in line, fares as badly, or worse, with his request for a
kiss: "May I, sweet lady, beg a kiss of you?"

> *Cressida.* You may.
> *Ulysses.*   I do desire it.
> *Cressida.*   Why, beg then.   [48]

She has caught the old fox with a very old trick: he has her
permission to beg a kiss, but that is all. Ulysses' attempt to re-
cover from this rebuff is less than impressive:

> Why then for Venus' sake, give me a kiss
> When Helen is a maid again and his.   [49–50]

Wit that should be crisp and salty is, instead, soggy and bitter.
Cressida fields this weakly hit ball tidily enough: "I am your
debtor, claim it when 'tis due." Since Helen is not likely to become a maid again or Menelaus', Cressida's is a not unwitty way

of saying that for her, never is a perfectly satisfactory time for Ulysses to claim his kiss. At this point Ulysses, exasperated because she has preempted his "Never," gives up trying to be witty and resorts to the statement direct: "Never's my day, and then a kiss of you." As Cressida is led away by Diomed, Nestor's exclamation, "A woman of quick sense," precipitates Ulysses' diatribe, of which I now give the whole:

> Fie, fie upon her!
> There's language in her eye, her cheek, her lip,
> Nay, her foot speaks; her wanton spirits look out
> At every joint and motive of her body.
> O, these encounterers, so glib of tongue
> That give [accosting] welcome ere it comes
> And wide unclasp the tables of their thoughts
> To every ticklish reader! set them down
> For sluttish spoils of opportunity,
> And daughters of the game.   [54–63]

If one looks at the written text of the scene, this seems simple assertion, unsupported by evidence.[22] The first lines merely describe any very sexually attractive girl as seen by a sour puritan; and the last lines are inaccurate. Cressida's presumably glib tongue has been silent until late in the action, and indeed she utters only a few more than seventy words in the whole scene. It is true that she manages to strike down Ulysses with thirteen of them, but it is not true that she has wide unclasped the tables of her thoughts to any reader less ticklish[23] than Ulysses. Nor has she given a welcome to accosting[24] before it comes, having received five kisses in total silence. Moreover, Ulysses' pluralization of Cressida, his multiplying her from an individual to a species, enables him to pin all the hypothetical sins of the species on her, the individual; as we might say: she's one of those girls who do such and such, or, in Elizabethan, Set her down as one of those sluttish spoils of opportunity and daughters of the game—you know the kind I mean. It seems clear that a pretty young woman should not defeat a middle-aged self-proclaimed thinker in a small battle of wits, or deny him a kiss that others have received. Sour are the grapes of his wrath.

In Cressida's last scene in the play (V.ii)—surely one of Shakespeare's greatest scenes—the ambiguity of her words persists, but is destroyed ultimately by the action. A multiplicity of viewers focus on her actions and words in this scene: she is talking with Diomed, and they are being watched from the deeper shadows by Troilus and Ulysses, and both couples are being watched from the deeper shadows by Thersites. All four men indicate by their comments that they think she is out to seduce Diomed, though perhaps all four of them, for their various reasons, are inclined to think seduction the chief occupation of an attractive woman. The scene almost amounts to a seminar on Cressida in which she is unanimously awarded the status of whoredom. Such public condemnation of her, combined with the dramatic compacting of the action, which seems to make the night of the scene the very next after the one in which Troilus and Cressida consummated their love, is very cruel to Shakespeare's heroine: Chaucer's was allowed to transfer her heart from Troilus to Diomede in relative privacy and with less shocking immediacy.

But Shakespeare's cruelty to Cressida does not much exceed Chaucer's to Criseyde in the matter of timing. In the poem, the culminating scene between Diomede and Criseyde takes place on the tenth evening after her departure from Troy (V 841–1029), the day by which she had promised Troilus she would return to the city. After Diomede leaves—his suit little discouraged by Criseyde's weak demurrals—she goes to bed in her father's tent and thinks about the words of "this sodaine Diomede"; and thus, according to the narrator, there "began to brede" the cause why she "toke fully purpose for to dwell." The next day, the eleventh after her leaving Troy, Diomede visits her again, and the narrator, while carefully avoiding a description of her final capitulation to Diomede, suddenly gets caught up in a summary of the action, with the result that, in a few brief stanzas, he takes us far into the future of their affair (V 1030–50). He tells quickly how Diomede comforted her and took away her cares, and lists the various amiable things that Criseyde did for the Greek warrior. This catalog concludes with the wonderfully anticlimatic remark, "Men saine—I not—that she yaue him her hart."[25] To this cruelly ironic bit of uncertainty—if, considering her other gifts, Criseyde had not given Diomede her heart she would indeed have become a whore—Shakespeare assigns a new but still cruel context. When his Cressida tells Diomed that he who takes from her the sleeve that Troilus had given her "doth take [her] heart withal," Diomed replies with blunt self-assurance, "I had your heart before."

Chaucer's narrator, apparently realizing that his summary of future action was damaging to his beloved lady, suddenly reverses direction and, with a touch of indignation, points out that it is not known how long it was before Criseyde accepted Diomede—he challenges the reader to find the time in any book in his library (1085–92). Unable to assign an authorized interval, he manages to suggest that it was a very long time, and then concludes with another horrid anticlimax. This is the wholly ambiguous statement that though Diomede "began to wooe her sone, / Er he her wan, yet was there more to done."[26] We are not told how much more. Having undone Criseyde by describing her future behavior, the narrator then undoes her more by trying to defend her, and ends up mortally undoing both his own defense and her. Shakespeare's cruelty is quick, Chaucer's long drawn out. A stanza after we leave Criseyde in the far-off future, we are returned to Troy, where it is still the ninth night after her departure and Troilus, still filled with hope of her return, is on the Troyan walls sighing his soul toward the Grecian tents.[27] The protracted disillusionment of Chaucer's Troilus is as harrowing in its own way as the sudden revelation to Shakespeare's Troilus of his love's perfidy, even though the latter virtually prophesied it.

In their final scenes, while both Criseyde and Cressida are a little like drained ponds, their former mysterious depths a mere memory and only pebbly shallows left to view, I think Cressida comes off a bit better than Criseyde. Criseyde, indeed, seems more like an inexperienced girl than the mature widow we thought we knew. Most girlish is her vow that, although she has "falsed" Troilus, to Diomede, at any rate, she will be true (1071). Her leisurely indecisiveness, so charming earlier when it concerned Troilus, now seems like the product of an irresponsible and self-deceiving nature, one simply incapable of facing herself squarely or making a firm decision, and so letting time decide for her. Her dishonest, though pathetic, attempt to explain herself to Diomede on the tenth day is a masterpiece of what Thersites would call juggling, especially in the way she dismisses Diomede while making sure he will return. She has just told him that her love for her late husband was the only love for which her heart had room, but then suggests that time might alter matters:

> To morow eke wol I speken with you fain
> So that ye touchen naught of this matere;
> And when you list ye may come here again.
> And er ye gon thus much I say you here:
> As helpe me Pallas with her heeres clere,
> If that I should of any Greke haue routh
> It should be yourseluen, by my trouth.
>
> I say nat therefore that I wol you loue,
> Ne say nat nay; but in conclusioun,
> I meane well, by God that sit aboue!   [995–1004]

To say "I mean well" is a final admission that one cannot cope with the crises of one's life, that the willingness to accept responsibility for one's actions is not large enough to bear the load that has been placed upon it. In Criseyde's later lament that her infidelity will make her a byword for female infamy in time to come, the exclamation, "Alas, that soch a caas me should fall" is the equivalent of the question Why did this have to happen to me? which is what one who is accepting the status of victim asks: Alas, alas, it's not my fault, so let time act, not me. Criseyde concludes with a nice speech of praise for Troilus, but with no recognition of her own responsibility for what has happened, despite the narrator's admiration for how sorry she felt about her untruth. Her last words, "But all shall passe, and thus take I my leaue" (1085), suggest that she has accepted the role of Fortune's woman.

Cressida's behavior at the time she yields to her new lover is to some extent déja vu: it will remind most readers of the scene in which she yields to Troilus. (In his handling of Criseyde's capitulation to Diomede, Chaucer's narrator also glances back at her earlier capitulation.)[28] Readers well-acquainted with the play are probably often influenced in their understanding of the earlier scene by the later: since in the later Cressida proves (whether she wants to or not) a successful coquette in that she keeps Diomed dancing in attendance, it is natural to argue that she was trying to keep Troilus doing the same when she threatened to leave the place because of her confusion and embarrassment. But just as it is possible to read the earlier scene, as I have done, as exemplifying sincerely felt impulses, so is it possible to read the second scene as not entirely excluding such impulses. Her effort to discourage Diomed may be a genuine, if fleeting one. Thersites thinks that Cressida's line, "Sweet honey Greek, tempt me no more to folly" (V.ii.18), is "Roguery," that is, mere flirtation. But it is not unambiguously roguery, and could be a sincere effort to lighten the pressure Diomed is putting upon her. When she says to him,

> I will not meet with you to-morrow night.
> I prithee, Diomed, visit me no more,   [73–74]

Thersites' comment is, "Now she sharpens. Well said, whetstone!" Yet she is taking a chance that Chaucer's Criseyde never takes: Chaucer's Criseyde asks Diomede not to speak to her of love (995–96), but does not at any time risk breaking off their relationship, as Cressida does. And, just as in the earlier scene such flirtatiousness as is often imputed to her saying "Stop my mouth" seems highly redundant, it is hard to see why Cressida supposes—as opposed to Thersites—that dismissing Diomed will bind him any more closely to her; he is obviously bound in his own predatory way as closely as could be. I rather suspect that Cressida really wishes she had the force of character—the unambiguousness—to make the dismissal stick. In any case, she seems more clearheaded about what she is doing than Criseyde, and when she gives the sleeve Troilus had given her to Diomed, she knows the full meaning of her gesture. "Come, tell me whose it was," he bids her. "'Twas one's that lov'd me better than you will," she answers, perhaps recalling Henryson, whose Diomeid finally casts Cresseid out. And in her final speech Cressida admits to the turpitude that Criseyde would not face.

In their last scenes both heroines let us and their former lovers down. The best Shakespearean comment on them both was long since applied to Cressida by Tucker Brooke:[29] "But yet the pity of it! . . . The pity of it!" Until her very last appearance, Cressida's ambiguity, like Criseyde's, persists, and because it does, she is at once unforgivable and one for whom, as for Chaucer's Criseyde, it is necessary to feel sympathy; and because she both is unforgivable and claims our sympathy, the play she is in, like Chaucer's poem before it, presents a vision sadder and deeper than such men as Ulysses, for all his wiliness, can see. And for us to see from the beginning of the play no potentiality in Cressida for a future better than the one we know she will have—something we grant readily to Chaucer's Criseyde—is to reduce the play's vision to that of Thersites. And that is a vision beyond faith, beyond hope, beyond the charity of the imagination, and beneath humanity.

6

Love and Laughter:
Troilus and Criseyde,
Romeo and Juliet,
the Wife of Bath,
and Falstaff

hen I first became interested in the relation of Chaucer to Shakespeare, it was the possible connection between *Troilus and Criseyde* and *Romeo and Juliet* on the one hand and between the Wife of Bath and Falstaff on the other that most engaged me. That was a number of years ago, and the sad fact is that the two connections remain to this day elusive, in many ways beyond my grasp. In my first chapter I pointed out how the authors of *Troilus* and *Romeo* handled melodramatic situations in somewhat the same manner, but a more tangible evidence of an influence that I am persuaded exists eludes me with the two love stories as with the two comic characters. Perhaps in both cases I should settle for analogy, or simple similarity, rather than influence. In that case I can take comfort in what Ann Thompson has written in her consideration of Shakespeare's possible use of *Troilus* in writing *Romeo and Juliet*: the question of whether or not this can be proved, she says, "need not take absolute precedence over the matter of whether it is valid and interesting to read these great works alongside each other. It is possible that to travel along this road is more important than to arrive."[1] I believe it is proper to extend her remark to include the very crooked road on which Falstaff and the Wife of Bath also traveled. In this chapter I hope that assuming an influence that cannot be proved may enable us at least to see in a new light certain aspects of the poem, the play, and the two characters.

Ann Thompson has written as well as anyone ever has on the subject of *Troilus and Criseyde* and *Romeo and Juliet*, and I start with her point that Shakespeare's play succeeded Chaucer's poem as "the single most important and influential love-tragedy in English poetry, the archetype to which situations in both life and literature [are] referred."[2] I should prefer to describe the poems as the two greatest love *poems* in English, rather than love-tragedies, even while emphasizing that they are both tragedies. But it is hard to think of a love-comedy that is comparable to either of these works, as the term love-tragedy suggests that there ought to be; the great love stories must, I guess, be sad. And thereby hangs a moral.

It is, however, a moral so obvious and so discouraging that I should like to defer discussion of it until later. For the moment I should like to make the point that neither the play nor the poem contains an even flatter and staler moral, which is that people should not fall so violently and passionately in love that they are willing to contravene the wishes of their parents (*Romeo and Juliet*) or go to bed with each other without getting married first (*Troilus and Criseyde*). That is, I do not think that the moral of either of these love stories is that one should not fall in love as intensely as at least three of the lovers in these works do. And in this negative point is one of the close similarities of the poem and the play, and their preeminent greatness as love stories.

The chief immediate source for Shakespeare's play, Arthur Brooke's *The Tragical Historye of Romeus and Juliet* is, according to its author, a negative moral exemplum. In a preface to the reader Brooke warns that he has written his "tragicall matter" because "the evill mans mischefe, warneth men not to be evyll."[3] Hence he will describe to us what happens to a

> coople of unfortunate lovers, thralling themselves to unhonest desire, neglecting the authoritie and advise of parents and frendes, conferring their principall counsels with dronken gossyppes, and superstitious friers (the naturally fitte instrumentes

of unchastitie) attemptyng all adventures of peryll, for thattay-
nyng of their wished lust, usyng auriculer confession (the kay of
whoredome, and treason) for furtherance of theyr purpose, abu-
syng the honorable name of lawefull mariage, [to] cloke the
shame of stolne contractes, finallye, by all means of unhonest
lyfe, hastyng to most unhappye deathe.

Romeus and Juliet is not a good poem (though not really as bad
as many commentators say it is), but it is, despite this horren-
dously disapproving prospectus, a very humane one. Indeed,
the tone of Brooke's prefatory note and the tone of the poem
itself are in total opposition. The poem shows almost nothing
but sympathy for the lovers, and that "naturally fit instrument
of unchastity," the friar, is a very nice man who, like his succes-
sor in Shakespeare, does his best to help the lovers stay honest,
as well as alive and happy. There are simply no evil people in
the poem by whose wickedness the reader is to be warned.
Brooke does his protestant duty by blaming it all on popery, but
he actually serves up not the nasty cake he promises but a rather
agreeable one.

Shakespeare, imitating what Brooke did and not what he said
he was doing, emphasizes the sadness of the story, but nowhere
suggests that it is a moral exemplum. The famous Prologue to
the play proposes to show "the misadventurous piteous over-
throws" of a "pair of star-cross'd lovers" and the "fearful passage of their death-mark'd love." It does not in any way condemn the lovers, but mentions how their sad fate finally brought
an end to their families' feud. In the last two lines of the play the
Prince offers his own simple summary,

> For never was a story of more woe
> Than this of Juliet and her Romeo.   [V.iii.309–10]

The spokesman for conventional morality within the play is
Friar Lawrence, but like everyone else he is so overwhelmed by
the rapidity with which events follow one another that he has
very little leisure for moralistic preachment. He stops both lovers in turn from suicide, but not with doctrinaire argument but
with the reasoning that they must continue to live in order not
to deprive the other of his beloved. Lust, part of Brooke's pro-

spectus, is of so little importance in the play that it is not mentioned. The lovers are in full agreement that they must marry
before they consummate their love. The moral weight of the
play, such as it is, is concentrated in the scene just before the
Friar weds the couple. His oft quoted speech—oft quoted because it has no rival in the play for moralization—is an answer
to Romeo's challenge to "love-devouring death" to do what it
dares so long as Romeo can call Juliet his own for just a moment. In an image that some scholars believe to have been borrowed from Chaucer's Criseyde's meditation, "Ful sharp beginning breaketh oft at ende" (II 791),[4] the Friar observes,

> These violent delights have violent ends,
> And in their triumph die, like fire and powder,
> Which as they kiss consume.   [II. vi. 9–11]

But after this generalization with its splendidly prophetic overtones, the Friar subsides into conventional moralization of the
drabbest sort, advising Romeo to love moderately, lest he grow
tired of Juliet:

> The sweetest honey
> Is loathsome in his own deliciousness,
> And in the taste confounds the appetite.
> Therefore love moderately: long love doth so;
> Too swift arrives as tardy as too slow.

This is simply the advice expected of a late medieval priest before he performs a marriage—indeed, one can't help recalling
Chaucer's Parson's sober (and sobering) advice to husbands to
love their wives with discretion, patiently, and attemperly (I
860). This piece of singularly ill-directed counsel is interrupted
by the sudden appearance of Juliet, who enchants the Friar out
of his parsonical persona just as he is sententiously observing
that "Too swift arrives as tardy as too slow." Her swift arrival
gives him the lie, and his moralization dissolves in appreciation:

> Here comes the lady. O, so light a foot
> Will ne'er wear out the everlasting flint.

From this mixture of unwitting prophecy and admiration of Juliet's grace he makes, or tries to make, a professional recovery:

> A lover may bestride the gossamers
> That idles in the wanton summer air,
> And yet not fall; so light is vanity.

Having marvelously suggested the buoyancy of young love—its ability to defy gravity—he twists the image of weightlessness into moral weightlessness, which is nothing, or vanity. But just as Friar Lawrence's moralization loses its way because of Juliet's charming appearance on the scene, so any attempt to read *Romeo and Juliet* as anything but a celebration of love must fail because of the great charm and intensity of the love affair and of the lovers: their weightlessness is not vanity. This is the last, weak effort Shakespeare allows Friar Lawrence to serve the play as Brooke's preface was supposed to serve the poem.

Brooke was familiar with Chaucer's *Troilus and Criseyde*, and it may be that his preface, so out of keeping with the tone of his poem, is a clumsy attempt to imitate the dichotomy that occasionally divides the narrator of Chaucer's poem from what the poem is saying, and does so especially in its ending. Like Shakespeare, Chaucer begins his work by stressing, indeed overstressing, its sadness, and making no mention of any moral content. The narrator proposes to tell of the "double sorrow" of Troilus in love, how his adventures "fell from woe to weal and after out of joy." He begins with verses so woeful that they weep as he writes them. He calls on the fury Tisiphone to serve as his muse, and she responds at once by helping him overwrite the second stanza of his poem so that its seven lines contain the nouns *torment* and *pain*, the verb *complain*, and the adjectives *cruel, woeful, dreary, sorry, sorrowing*, and *sorrowful* (twice)—an exercise in verbal agony that threatens to drown in its own tears.

But once he has established himself in the first fifty-six lines as the translator of a very sad story and has warned the reader in so many words that Criseyde forsook Troilus before she died, he goes on merrily cheering the principal characters into their love affair and occasionally giving very dubious advice, such as that the ladies in his audience should yield to their lovers as Criseyde finally did to Troilus. There is neither sadness nor morality. For three-fifths of the way through, the story is told as one of romantic sexual love that's going to end splendidly, and the full force of the sadness does not assert itself until the final book. It is only after the narrator has shown us Criseyde accepting Diomede in Troilus' place and Troilus' finally being persuaded of her betrayal that the narrator begins to worry about the morality of his story. This he does after Troilus is killed by Achilles and ascends to the eighth sphere (the seventh, according to the black-letter editions). From there Troilus looks down upon this little spot of earth, laughs at those who weep for his death, and damns all our work that so follows "this blinde lust." And the narrator goes on to exhort "yonge fresshe folkes, he or she" in whom love grows up with their years to love Christ, who will not betray them, and to seek no "feigned" loves (V 1842–48).

This is, of course, a moral with a vengeance, one that converts an 8,200-line poem in praise of love into a negative moral exemplum fifty lines from its end—a tiny tail of extraordinary moral weightiness wagging a huge shaggy dog. In Chaucer criticism, this tiny tail is commonly given the name "Chaucer" to distinguish it from the huge dog "Narrator," to which it is attached. To excuse the imbalance between the two entities, which in its own statistical way is as gross as Brooke's preface is to his poem, it is possible to conjure up at least the wraith of a moral appearing earlier in the poem: Chaucer's narrator does describe his poem as a tragedy, and it is well known that a medieval tragedy always has a moral (and always the same moral), and that the moral of medieval tragedy is at least conformable with Chaucer's advice to young people to restrain themselves from loving one another.

There is some force in this proposition, though I do not think it quite justifies reading the poem as a negative moral exemplum, written to discourage romantic love. Everyone in Chaucer's medieval audience knew what to expect of a tragedy, and though Chaucer does not actually tell us that he is writing a tragedy until about eighty lines from its end (V 1786)—after he has written it, really—the very first stanza of the poem, summarizing Troilus' falling from woe to weal in his love affair, and afterward out of joy, suggests by its terminology that the poem is to be a medieval tragedy, though the fall from woe to weal is against normal tragic gravity. Our most reliable expert on medieval tragedy is, of course, Chaucer's Monk, who defines it as a story such as we find in old books of those who stood in great prosperity and fell out of it, ending wretchedly (B^2 3165–67). The Monk's negative exempla teach us, again and again, that this world is governed by the fickle Lady Fortune, who allows some people to ride high on her Ferris wheel for a time but then inevitably hurls them down into the slough, where they end wretchedly. The moral, and a mighty paltry moral it is, is "Fortune will get you in the end." Notice that the moral character of the protagonist (or victim) is not at issue: Nero makes as good a tragic hero as someone far more worthy. To qualify for a tragedy, all one has to do is rise high and fall, and the tragic quotient is determined by the altitude from which one falls.

As defined and practiced by the Monk—and by a number of writers in the Middle Ages, including Boccaccio—tragedy is without doubt the most flaccid literary form that ever gave a writer an excuse to tell a sad story. The morals appended to the *Gesta Romanorum* have at least variety in their idiocy, even if they share the vacuity of the endlessly repeated tragic morals. But there is, of course, a more grown-up form of medieval tragedy than the Monk's. Instead of simply reviling Fortune, its moral warns: "Do not *commit* yourself to Fortune." What this amounts to is a recommendation of a certain wary stoicism—be prepared for the worst and try not to put your whole being into something that may not last; meanwhile, derive what comfort you can from bad experience, and enjoy the good. In Dante and above all in Boethius, Fortune assumes a philosophical dimension of some stature, with at least an educational message for those whom Fortune has spurned.

But is Chaucer's poem a representative of either one of these variations of medieval tragedy, the Monk's or Boethius'? Well, it fits the Monk's, but gains little by doing so. Troilus is a person of high degree who for a time enjoys felicity with Criseyde, then loses her by an act of Fortune, and ends wretchedly. And one might say that the Monk and the narrator of *Troilus* are alike in that both spend more time recounting the good things the protagonists enjoyed while they were high on the wheel than they do on their wretched endings. But unlike *The Monk's Tale*, where the good things are merely material, the love of Troilus and Criseyde has enormous spiritual urgency; we recognize in it a potentiality of life at its very best. And Chaucer varies from his Monk in that he gives Fortune's wheel a symbolic last turn when, after his death, Troilus is sent up to what seems to me unquestionably a better place (though it is open to question)[5] than this world, there to reside, presumably, permanently. This is a violation of the Monk's tragic rules, which allow no dealings with the afterlife. Chaucer's poem is only most superficially a tragedy in the Monk's sense.

I must digress here for a moment to deal with a matter related to the subject of tragedy that keeps coming up in criticism even though it has no right to. That is, the possibility that the narrator's injunction to "yonge, fresshe folkes, he or she" to place their hearts in Christ rather than in "feigned" loves somehow has application to the lovers Troilus and Criseyde. The medieval proclivity for anachronism is, I admit, outrageous, often worse than Shakespeare's. Criseyde swears by God more often than any other woman in Chaucer, and it is clearly the Christian God by whom the narrator thinks she is swearing. But this is merely to bring a highborn Trojan lady up-to-date for fourteenth-century Londoners, and not to make her a proleptic Christian. It is not at all the same thing as equipping ancient Troy with the full doctrine of the medieval Church, complete with patristic exegetes. Despite his frequent use of Christian ideas in the story he is telling, the narrator is perfectly aware that the Trojan gods were Jove, Apollo, Mars, and such rascaille, and he curses them roundly at the end for not taking better care of Troilus. Troilus simply did not have a god worthy of being given his heart. In the same realm of improbability is the argument that Troilus and Criseyde were guilty of mortal sin because they committed fornication—some critics accuse them of adultery, apparently feeling that adultery has more hamartialogical dignity than fornication.[6] Troilus and Criseyde knew nothing of Christianity or of medieval restrictions on sex, and are not liable to Christian judgment.

But to return to the moral of medieval tragedy in its relation to the poem. The Boethian lesson of not committing oneself does apply to Troilus, but only obliquely and awkwardly. For it is not Fortune that Troilus commits himself to so much as it is Criseyde. In his naughtier moments Chaucer does play with the idea that Criseyde is Dame Fortune: at the beginning of Book IV, in outlining the remainder of the plot, his narrator trembles at the thought of relating how Fortune turned her bright face away from Troilus and took no heed of him,

> But caste him clene out of his ladies grace,
> And on her whele she set vp Diomede.   [IV 10–11]

Here the woman Fortune's casting Troilus out of the woman Criseyde's grace and setting up Diomede on her wheel is a maneuver that the mind is much tempted to simplify by having Criseyde do her own casting out and setting up. And Criseyde's final words in the poem, her farewell to the absent Troilus, "But all shall passe, and thus take I my leave" (V 1085), are a kind of identification of herself with Fortune. Yet to press the matter too hard, as Chaucer knew, would be to reduce the poem to an antifeminist allegory drained of its lifeblood: an allegory of a paradise in which for Troilus, as for Adam, every prospect pleases and only Eve is vile. Chaucer is always aware that the plot of his story is one of the great showpieces of antifeminism, and he is careful not to let the issue come to the surface—despite moments when it comes very close to the surface. Still, the poem's moral is not, Don't trust a woman, which is the moral that comes into being if one allows the full identification of Criseyde with Fortune.

But even if one rejects—as I do—all these candidates, the poem does have a moral. This moral, I reiterate, can have no ex post facto application to Troilus and Criseyde, and it is simply that the best thing we know, love, is unreliable, like all things human. If you wish to ensure constancy in love, you had better love God, who will betray none who loves him. And this is true enough. I have argued elsewhere that the tiny tail we call Chaucer in the ending of the poem is not really a separate entity from the big dog we call narrator, but is the narrator's own proper tail.[7] Heartbroken over the way his poem has come out (as if he had forgotten the end of the story despite his having warned us of it in the overly emotional beginning), the narrator again reacts violently and overemotionally. He jumps to the conclusion that no love affair will work out, hence get thee to a nunnery or a monastery, go. I think many of us, myself included, have been too anxious to separate the narrator from the poet Chaucer. Actually, the huge dog is a hybrid, consisting of a poet who sees the beauty in romantic love and a poet who sees its instability, and they've been working together all the way through. The one we call narrator takes the more extreme position in favor of love, and now that it's let him down, he takes the more extreme position in its dispraise. Although the universalizing effect of great art suggests that because this love affair did not work out, no love affair so intense, so consuming, so lovely will work out, I still very much doubt that the alternative that is suggested to falling in love, a life of celibacy and human lovelessness, is one that Chaucer expected many of his young, fresh readers to choose. They would surely ask themselves in what sense Troilus would have been better off *not* to fall in love with Criseyde. World-hating is a medieval occupation, but richness of experience is a timeless need.

And this brings us back to Shakespeare. For the moral—which is not quite the right word—of *Romeo and Juliet* is the same as that of *Troilus and Criseyde*: love at its most passionate and its most fulfilling does not last in the real world. Romeo and Juliet never had a chance of making a go of it over a longer period of time than the play's brief duration, not even a chance to equal the longer but still brief happiness allotted to Troilus and Criseyde. In neither case is the sad denouement the result of moral principles asserting themselves in opposition to the loves of the characters. Shakespeare's tragedy is more tragic—and more satisfactory—because it is the lovers that the world destroys, not their love. In Chaucer's poem the love is flawed in the person of Criseyde—a much more interesting person than

Juliet, but not the stuff of which tragic heroines are made. She cannot sustain the dizzying and unreal rapture of such lovers as Troilus and Juliet and Romeo. Shakespeare, replacing what was the greatest love poem in English with what is the greatest love poem in English, eliminated the traces of medieval antifeminism and made the tragic symmetry perfect. But both poets wrote magnificent celebrations of love, and I can hardly think of anything better to celebrate.

From the sublime to the ridiculous—the sublimely ridiculous. We can never ascertain whether Shakespeare had the Wife of Bath in mind—at least in his unconscious mind—when he created Falstaff.[8] It may be merely a coincidence that Falstaff in one of his early appearances is seen on the pilgrim route to Canterbury; and it may have been merely Shakespeare's instinct that told him that a gross solipsist of enormous vitality would be the proper comic figure to provide an anti-heroic foil for a fledgling monarch and an ironic commentary on the values of English power politics, and that he never thought of that earlier large solipsist of enormous vitality who provides a foil for all the virtuous wives in fact and fiction and an ironic commentary on the Middle Ages' received ideas about marriage and the nature of women. The ironic commentaries that Falstaff and the Wife of Bath make are, because of the assurance and authority of their personalities, as persuasive as is the reality of the milieus in which they live and to which they respond. Both are supremely self-confident in their idiosyncrasy. As is often pointed out, they both use—or rather misuse—in their own defense the verse of St. Paul in the first Epistle to the Corinthians, in which he enjoins Christ's followers to remain in that vocation to which they have been called. Speaking of her total dedication to the vocation of matrimony, the Wife announces

> In such a state as god hath cleped vs
> I wol perseuer: I nam not precious.   [D 147–48]

And when the Prince comments on Falstaff's role as a taker of purses, Falstaff replies, "Why, Hal, 'tis my vocation, Hal, 'tis no sin for a man to labor in his vocation" (I.ii.104–05). I am not suggesting that Shakespeare needed the Wife of Bath to put St. Paul's text into Falstaff's mind, for the verse from the Epistle is one of several Pauline texts that were probably often perverted in a way that would have horrified the Apostle. In the C-text of *Piers Plowman*, for example, Long Will beats off an attack by Conscience and Reason on his begging his bread for a living by citing the verse as an excuse for not performing manual labor.[9] All three characters are suggesting, with varying degrees of seriousness, that, although others may find what they do reprehensible, they find their occupations fully jusitifed because they are *their* occupations, and they find them congenial. Their ideas of the world may be at variance with other people's ideas, but they are at home with them, and do not intend to alter their styles for anyone. And, if I may pervert Scripture myself, they speak not as the Scribes and Pharisees, but as those having authority.

Judith Kollmann has recently pointed out a number of similarities between *The Canterbury Tales* and *The Merry Wives of Windsor*,[10] and I myself wonder if that play does not make a backhanded acknowledgment of Shakespeare's awareness of *The Wife of Bath*. The merry wives are in many ways, not including wifely virture, like the Wife of Bath—independent, resourceful, sturdy women of the same middle-class background as she. This is, indeed, as Professor Kollmann shows, a background one associates with Chaucer's *Canterbury Tales* and hardly at all with Shakespeare's plays, which are mostly aristocratic or upper class, with bits of low life thrown in for spice. But the community of Windsor is made up of the same sort of people as the community of the Canterbury pilgrims, and is complete with the Host of the Garter Inn, whose involvement with what is going on around him is like that of the Host of the Tabard Inn, who leads the Canterbury pilgrims. The two wives of the play administer sorely needed lessons about women to two men, a jealous husband and an unlikely courtly lover, and this is an enterprise that the Wife of Bath would have cheered them on in, especially when they punished that most porcine of male chauvinist pigs, Sir John Falstaff, who had the gall to rival her in comic grandeur. And indeed, the punishment of Falstaff is effected by facsimiles of those very fairies whom the Wife of Bath tells us the Friar has blessed out of existence—one of whom teaches a lesson about women to the young rapist in *The Wife of Bath's Tale.*

Of the many traits the Wife of Bath and Falstaff share, one of the most striking is their wit. Of Falstaff, who boasts that the brain of man "is not able to invent anything that intends to laughter more than I invent or is invented upon me," and that he is "not only witty in [him]self, but the cause that wit is in other men" (*Henry IV Part 2*, I.ii.7–10), no more need be said— though it's tempting to say it anyhow. But the Wife's wit is sometimes underestimated. She is, for instance, a past-mistress of the progressively engulfing squelch, the insult that hurts the victim more the more he thinks about it. At the end of a tirade directed at one of her doddering husbands she asks him, out of the blue, "What aileth soche an old man for to chide?" (D 281). Perhaps one has to be a man of advanced—or advancing—years really to feel how this question goes on subtly cutting deeper after the first superficial wound has been felt: apparently old age cancels a man's right to complain about anything, especially a vigorous wife, for an old man ought, she implies, to feel noth- ing but gratitude for being allowed to clutter up the house with his useless carcass. One does not have to be a friar to savor the wit of her devastating repayment of the Friar on the pilgrimage for his patronizing comments on her learning and the length of her prologue. She explains that the friars, having blessed fairies out of existence, have taken their place: the result is that women may walk the countryside safely, for where there used to be an incubus there is now only a friar, and he'll do nothing to women—except dishonor them (857–81).

As the quotation from St. Paul suggests, both the Wife of Bath and Falstaff are adept at converting received *dicta*, whether biblical or proverbial, into slightly askew statements critical of other people's values or expressive of their own. I say "convert- ing," for the process is not really one of twisting such texts as it is reinterpreting them by a surprising use of logic. That human flesh is frail is an observation so trite that it has lost its force as a moral warning and has become an extenuating statement. Or so

Falstaff suggests when he restates it in the comparative degree: "Thou seest I have more flesh than another man, and therefore more frailty" (*Henry IV Part 1*, III.iii.166–68). "The lion will not touch the true prince" is a statement which, under Falstaff's analysis, serves to excuse Falstaff's unlion-like failure to oppose Hal and Poins when they rob him of the booty of the Gadshill theft, and also to validate both Hal's claim to be a true prince and Falstaff's to be a lion, whose instinct caused him to run away from his sovereign (II.iv.270–75). The Wife of Bath, though her *forte* is the Bible—to which I shall return—matches this refurbishment of an adage by her reinterpretation of the innocent little saying that it is too miserly for a man to refuse to let another man light a candle at his lantern, since he'll have none the less light as a result (D 333–34). When the Wife identifies the man as a husband and the lantern as his wife, the proverb takes on shocking implications, managing to justify a wife's extramarital sexual activity while dutifully preserving the medieval tenet that the wife is the husband's chattel, like any other of his tangible goods.

The Wife of Bath and Falstaff create their individual versions of reality by the protraction of their speech: they erect large verbal structures which fill the listener's mind and exclude from it all other matter. The prologue to the Wife's tale is approximately as long as the Prologue to *The Canterbury Tales*, a proportionment in which she would have found nothing to criticize. In all three of the plays in which Falstaff appears one finds long, long prose passages spoken by Falstaff, sometimes to someone else, but more often to himself, and us. He is a soliloquist more copious than Hamlet. Yet despite the fact that these solipsistic monologists are constantly explaining themselves to us, we are often not sure where to have them. Both make ironic commentaries on their milieus, but both also *are* ironic commentaries on their milieus, and as such they share, along with irony, the effect of making the reader uncertain of the exact locus from which their speeches proceed—their *locus loquendi*, if I may invent a critical term. Sturdy no-nonsense commonsense is the basis for one of their guises, though this can at any time modulate into almost frightening sophistication. And both guises can suddenly give way to childlike naivete—the kind of thing that enables the child in the old story to see that the emperor has no clothes on. And occasionally both seem genuinely naive, becoming parodies of adult behavior in the same way that small children are. One might say that the Wife of Bath and Falstaff share a Wordsworthian child's vision, uncluttered by conventions, with intimations of immorality. And each has a fourth guise as well, though one they do not share: the Wife's is the ferocious aggressive intensity of the shrew, while Falstaff's, rather surprisingly, is that of injured innocence.

Chaucer is careful to confirm our impression of the Wife of Bath's instability of guise when, after the Pardoner's interruption, she consents to his request that she teach him about marriage with an apology, which under the color of clarification produces obfuscation:

> . . . I pray to al this company
> If that I speke after my fantasy
> As taketh not agrefe of that I say,
> For mine entent is not but to playe.   [D 189–92]

We know precisely what the meanings of the word *fantasy* are, but unfortunately we do not know which of the two dominant meanings is the right one. Serious scholars—over-serious, in my opinion—have suggested that she means by *fantasy* imagination, not delight and, hence, that the whole story of her marriages is a fabrication, just as she tells us that her version of what her old husbands used to say to her when they came home drunk is a fabrication. But to deny that the Wife's account of her marriages is true is to raise the insuperable problem of evaluating the truth of a fiction in relation to the truth of a fiction within a fiction. Are the separate stories in *Don Quixote* more or less true than the story of *Don Quixote*? And, in order to complicate matters, the Wife does not quite say that she is speaking after her fantasy, but asks her hearers not to be offended *if* she speaks after her fantasy: we do not know when, if ever, the protasis of the conditional sentence begins to govern the discourse. Chaucer has been careful to give the Wife of Bath's ironies an elusiveness that makes them seem to be in perpetual motion.

The Wife tells us that her intent is only to play, and that is perhaps true most of the time of Falstaff. But as with the Wife, we are often unsure where his play begins or leaves off. The most obvious example is at the tavern after the Gadshill robbery. When Falstaff boasts of his heroic behavior, and in doing so multiplies two rogues in buckram suits into eleven and then adds three misbegotten knaves in Kendall green (II.iv.191–224), does he really expect the Prince and Poins to believe him? Actually, the question is easily answered, but answered, unhappily, as easily in the negative as in the affirmative. For Falstaff's expectations are as obscure as those of Chaucer's Pardoner, when, after fully exposing his fraudulence, he tries at the end of his tale to get the Host to buy some of his pardon (C 919–59). Critical argument is unending about whether the Pardoner really thought he could make a sale. The Host's furious response reflects his ill ease, because the Pardoner is a user and exemplifier of irony whose center the Host cannot locate. The reader is apt to be similarly ill at ease with Falstaff, and critics occasionally imitate the Host's treatment of the Pardoner by trying to reduce Falstaff's various guises to mere matter, and to gross matter at that. In a way, that is what Hal is forced to do when he finally rejects Falstaff. He did not overhear Falstaff's catechism on honor at Shrewsbury (V.i.129–41), but as King he would recognize that such playful subversions are more dangerous to his rule than any robberies at Gadshill, despite, or perhaps because of, the catechism's taking the elementary form of a schoolboy's lesson. Such an ambiguously motivated question of Falstaff's when he learns that the party they are about to rob at Gadshill consists of eight or ten men, as "'Zounds, will they not rob us?" (II.ii.65) may appear on the printed page as pure play. But spoken, it develops ambiguity. Should one say, "Will they not *rob* us?" like an honest man fearing to fall among thieves, or "Will *they* not rob *us*?" like a thief recognizing that there may be other thieves with superior numbers?

And what is one to make—and what did Hal make?—of Falstaff's soliloquy just before the robbery, which is overheard by the Prince?

Well, I doubt not but to die a fair death for all this, if I scape hanging for killing that rogue [Prince Hal]. I have forsworn his company hourly any time this two and twenty years, and yet I am bewitch'd with the rogue's company. If the rascal have not given me medicines to make me love him, I'll be hanged. It could not be else, I have drunk medicines. [II.ii.13–20]

In order to put a consistently cynical and knowing base under Falstaff so he can be pinned down, critics have suggested that he knows Prince Hal is listening, and that he is saying what will ingratiate himself with him. But this is to explain a mystery by denying it existence. It is really another irony that the love of Falstaff for the Prince is real, though it is expressed here at once with a childlike naiveté and in the ironical language Falstaff often uses in public, with the reason for his love being assigned to, even blamed on, the Prince, a rogue who he feels has corrupted him. Is there some chance that the "reverent vice," as the Prince calls him, really has a heart that is suitable for a "goodly portly man, i' faith, and a corpulent, of a cheerful look, a pleasing eye, and a most noble carriage" (II.iv.421–23) as Falstaff describes himself? Perhaps.

The Wife of Bath's bases are equally troublesome. Her approach to the Bible and its commentators is a combination of naive literalism, a somewhat questioning sense of reverence, and plain commonsense grounded in experience. She has trouble, as moralistic critics are always pointing out, understanding that it is not the letter but the spirit that one must heed. The relevant significance of Christ's remark to the Samaritan women at the well, "Thou hast had five husbands and that man that now hath thee is not thy husband" (D 14–25), eludes her. And well it might. The proposition, of which she has been told, that the text somehow limits the number of husbands a woman can have to five (six being over the legal limit) stems from St. Jerome, who heaped his Pelion of antifeminism upon the antifeminist Ossa of St. Paul. St. Jerome's proposition was based on his misreading of the biblical story, a confusion worse confounded by the Wife when she fails to understand that Christ was referring not to a fifth husband, but to a sixth man to whom the Samaritan woman had said she was not married—a disclaimer suppressed by St. Jerome in his eagerness to see that his reading of the spirit should not be belied by the letter.[11] The tenuousness of such blatantly prejudiced spiritual readings of the Bible is equally reflected in the Wife of Bath's natural perplexity and the saint's willful inaccuracy. The absurdity is enhanced by the Wife's attempt to fit the proposition to herself by misreading St. Jerome's misreading, so that the number of husbands comes out to four plus one questionable one, instead of five plus one man unwedded. Five is her current total if, as she carefully says, the fifth was canonically legal. But she herself can think of no explanation for Christ's choice of the number four, and seems ultimately to decide that the number of consecutive husbands she may have is unlimited.

In dealing with St. Paul, the Wife uses a literalist approach worthy of a puritan reformer. She reminds him of his admission that on the subject of matrimony he had no higher authority (79–82). And she uses those texts that please her and lets the others go without notice. She knows that her husband should leave father and mother and take only unto her (30–31), and that she has power over her husband's body and not he (158–59), but she fails to mention any reciprocal obligation. Yet in so doing she is providing a naturally ironic commentary on generations of celibate experts on marriage, who endlessly repeat the woman's obligation and rarely mention the husband's. She is understandably uncertain why, if the patriarchs had a number of wives, multiplicity of spouses is now deemed reprehensible (55–58). She envies Solomon his many spouses, and suppresses—if she is aware of it—the fact that Solomon's uxoriousness in building temples to his wives' strange gods brought the Lord's wrath down on him (35–43).

She even performs a bit of sophisticated biblical interpretation of her own: first she wishes that she had Solomon's gift from God of being "refreshed" by spouses as often as he was (37–38); later she remarks that she is willing to let virgins be bread of pure wheat seed and wives barley bread; but finally she notes that with barley bread Christ "refreshed" many a man (143–46)—a mixture of letter and spirit that would do credit to a patristic, intellectually speaking, if not morally. Her culminating combining of simplicity and sophistication occurs in her lament, "Alas, alas, that euer loue was sin!" (614). Moralists sometimes seize on this as proof that the Wife was aware of her sinfulness and regretted it. But her apparent repentance is actually parody, a parody of the repentance one is led to expect. It is not Christian remorse that provokes her exclamation, but regret that because sexual love is sin its availability to her has been reduced. An old age of repentance is no more the Wife of Bath's prospectus than it ever was Falstaff's.

Both the Wife of Bath and Falstaff are, though utterly charming, perfectly horrible people. It is true that the Wife's victims are mostly husbands who deserved the abuse and exploitation she practiced on them. But she is a habitual fornicator and adulterer, and her ability to be disagreeable when her authority is challenged is not limited to the domestic scene, as any parish wife who gets to the Offering before her learns. Falstaff is not only a drunken old man, but a thief, a deadbeat, an exploiter of poor women and shallow justices from whom he borrows money that he fails to repay, an abuser of the King's press, a lecher, a liar, and heaven knows what else. And as two very dubious citizens, they should *not* be sentimentalized. I say this very sternly, for I am aware that I can never discuss them at length without sentimentalizing them. I blame this on their creators, who seem to have loved them dearly while endowing them with enough vices to supply an army of the wicked— enough vices and enough vitality. I have always supposed that *Henry IV Part 2* exists largely because Falstaff's vitality was too bountiful to be confined in *Part 1*; and surely *The Merry Wives of Windsor* exists because of him. Shakespeare originally promised that Falstaff would show up in *Henry V* (Epilogue to *Henry IV Part 2*), but prudently changed his mind and killed him off before he could stop Hal from ever getting to Agincourt. The Wife of Bath managed to get herself into *The Merchant's Tale* (E 1685– 87) and into Chaucer's "Envoy to Bukton"—also an unruly fiction who would not remain on the page where she belonged. Both characters took on life independent of their creators.

And both are associated with passages of unrivaled emotional

effectiveness, passages that are as splendid tributes to human vitality as any I know. The Wife of Bath speaks hers, and Falstaff's
is spoken about him. The Wife of Bath's is a digression from her
account of her fourth husband:

> My fourth husbonde was a reuelour—
> This is to saie, he had a paramour.
> And I was yong, and full of ragerie,
> Stubburne and strong, and ioly as a Pie.
> Well coud I daunce to an Harpe smale,
> And sing, iwis, as a Nitingale,
> Whan I had dronken a draught of swete wine.
> Metellus, the foule churle, the swine,
> That with a staffe biraft his wife her life
> For she dronk wine, though I had be his wife,
> He should not haue daunted me fro drinke.
> And after wine of Venus must I thinke,
> For also seker as cold engendreth haile,
> A likorus mouth must haue a lecherous taile.
> In women vinolent is no defence:
> This knowe lecherous by experience.
>
> But lord Christ, when it remembreth me
> Vpon my youth and my iolite,
> It tickleth me about the hart roote—
> Vnto this daie is doeth my hart boote—
> That I haue had my worlde as in my time.
> But age, alas, that all woll enuenime
> Hath me biraft my beaute and my pith.
> Let go, fare well, the deuile go therwith!
> The floure is gon, ther nis no more to tell;
> The bran, as I best can, now mote I sell.
> But yet to be right merie woll I fonde.
> Now forth to tell of my fourth husbonde.   [D 453–80]

I doubt that many who have spent their lives far better than the
Wife are able to look back with such a sense of benediction as
that with which the Wife of Bath looks back on her misspent
past. She has enjoyed life, and will go on enjoying it. And although she is a very immoral woman, she has, in her enjoyment, perfect integrity.

Perhaps Falstaff was incapable of so philosophical a looking back—that was not one of his guises. But Shakespeare gives him the same kind of emotional justification in the erstwhile Mistress Quickly's account of his death in *Henry V*, a kind of apology by the dramatist for Hal's shabby treatment of him and the merry wives' triumph over him. In the scene, Bardolph has just reacted violently to Falstaff's death, wishing he were "with him, wheresome'er he is, either in heaven or hell." The Hostess replies:

> Nay sure, he's not in hell; he's in Arthur's bosom, if ever man went to Arthur's bosom. 'A made a finer end, and went away and it had been any christom child. 'A parted ev'n just between twelve and one, ev'n at the turning o' th' tide; for after I saw him fumble with the sheets, and play with flowers, and smile upon his finger's end, I knew there was but one way; for his nose was as sharp as a pen, and 'a [talk'd] of green fields. "How now, Sir John?" quoth I, "what, man? be a' good cheer." So 'a cried out, "God, God, God!" three or four times. Now I, to comfort him, bid him 'a should not think of God; I hop'd there was no need to trouble himself with any such thoughts yet. So 'a bade me lay more clothes on his feet. I put my hand into the bed and felt them, and they were as cold as any stone; then I felt to his knees, [and they were as cold as any stone;] and so up'ard and up'ard, and all was as cold as any stone.[12]

Both passages occur in marvelously comic contexts, and both are perfectly controlled in their tone, with the pathos not spoiling the humor, or vice versa. I don't think we should worry about the Hostess' misplacement of Falstaff in Arthur's bosom, any more than we should worry about the final destination of the wife of Bath's soul—*she* never did. Both characters are in any case still very much alive, very much their creators' celebrations of life, and I can hardly think of anything better to celebrate.

Notes

Introduction

1 "Chaucer and Shakespeare," *Quarterly Review*, 134 (1873), 225–55.
2 Nevill Coghill, "Shakespeare's Reading in Chaucer," *Elizabethan and Jacobean Studies Presented to F. P. Wilson*, ed. Herbert Davis and Helen Gardner (Oxford: Oxford University Press, 1959), pp. 86–99. Coghill fails to discuss *Troilus*, and while he leads the reader to suppose that he will discuss wider issues, he actually is most preoccupied with the kinds of details that show Shakespeare's acquaintance with Chaucer.
3 Ann Thompson, *Shakespeare's Chaucer: A Study in Literary Origins* (Liverpool: Liverpool University Press, 1978).
4 Dorothy Bethurum [Loomis], "Shakespeare's Comment on Mediaeval Romance in *Midsummer Night's Dream*," *MLN*, 60 (1945), 85–94.
5 Philip Edwards, "On the Design of *The Two Noble Kinsmen*," *REL*, 5 (1964), 89–105. Clifford Leech, in his Signet edition, *William Shakespeare and John Fletcher*, *The Two Noble Kinsmen* (New York: The New American Library, 1966), pp. 187–91.
6 C. S. Lewis, *The Allegory of Love* (Oxford: Oxford University Press, 1936), pp. 176–91.
7 Kenneth Muir, *The Sources of Shakespeare's Plays* (New Haven: Yale University Press, 1978), p. 143.
8 Muir (*Sources*, p. 144): ". . . in Chaucer's poem he [Diomede] is a noble warrior who wins Criseyde by his long and eloquent wooing."

Chapter 1

1 Quotations from Chaucer are from Stow's 1561 printing of Thynne's edition of 1532, with punctuation modernized. Line numbers are those of the standard modern texts.
2 Quotations from *A Midsummer Night's Dream* are from the new Arden edition, ed. Harold F. Brooks (London: Methuen, 1979). Incidental quotations from Shakespearean plays not under primary consideration

are, throughout this book, from *The Riverside Shakespeare*, ed. G. B. Evans et al. (Boston: Houghton Mifflin, 1974).

3 G. K. Chesterton, *Chaucer* (London: Faber & Faber, 1932; new ed. 1948), p. 19.

4 Bethurum, "Shakespeare's Comment," pp. 85–94, especially p. 90. Bethurum's suggestion was ultimately adopted by Nevill Coghill, despite his earlier having taken a rather dim view of her article: see *Shakespeare's Professional Skills* (Cambridge: Cambridge University Press, 1964), p. 56, and cf. Coghill's "Shakespeare's Reading in Chaucer," p. 91.

5 In *Sources and Analogues of Chaucer's Canterbury Tales*, ed. W. F. Bryan and Germaine Dempster (Chicago: University of Chicago Press, 1941), pp. 486–559.

6 Kenneth Muir, "Pyramus and Thisbe: A Study in Shakespeare's Method," *SQ*, 5 (1954), 141–53; *Shakespeare's Sources* (London: Methuen, 1957), pp. 31–47; and *Sources*, pp. 66–77: references are to the last of these unless otherwise noted. See also *Narrative and Dramatic Sources of Shakespeare*, ed. Geoffrey Bullough (New York: Columbia University Press, 1957), I, 373–76, and David P. Young, *Something of Great Constancy* (New Haven: Yale University Press, 1966), pp. 32–48. Thompson (*Shakespeare's Chaucer*, pp. 88–94) notes no more Chaucerian echoes in the artisans' play than those pointed out by Muir and others.

7 Katherine Duncan-Jones, "Pyramus and Thisbe: Shakespeare's Debt to Mouffet Cancelled," *RES NS*, 32 (1981), 296–301. Although it has always been acknowledged that Mouffet's poem was not published until after Shakespeare's play had been written, Duncan-Jones finds evidence that it was not written until after the play had appeared.

8 See Muir, *Sources*, p. 72; but in his edition, p. 120, Brooks notes that *pap* had been used elsewhere with males.

9 In his edition, p. 121, Brooks has an excellent discussion of the gender of Thisbe's epithets for Pyramus.

10 Muir, *Sources*, p. 73.

11 Ibid., p. 72.

12 Ibid., p. 74.

13 Both occurrences are in *The Merry Wives of Windsor*, a play with possible Chaucerian connections. See chapter 6.

14 Chaucer's list had included the dubiously musical woodpigeon ("wodedouve"), for which several late manuscripts and the printed editions stemming from Thynne substituted the wholly unmusical woodcock: Shakespeare would have none of this joke.

15 Muir, *Sources*, pp. 70–71.

16 As Muir points out (*Sources*, p. 73), Shakespeare's Pyramus calls the wall "wicked" at V.i.178. In his 1957 edition of *Sources*, p. 38, Muir suggests that the lion's "bloody mouth" (V.i.142) may have been taken from Chaucer's lion's "blody mouth" (*Legend of Good Women*, line 807).

17 For the best discussion of the two poets in relation to one another, see
    Eleanor J. Winsor [Leach], "A Study of the Sources and Rhetoric of
    Chaucer's *Legend of Good Women* and Ovid's *Heroides*," Ph.D. diss., Yale
    University, 1968; see also the fine study by John M. Fyler, *Chaucer and
    Ovid* (New Haven: Yale University Press, 1979), pp. 96–123. The hu-
    morous side of Chaucer's narratives of abused women is often missed:
    Muir remarks (*Sources*, p. 72) that Chaucer's version of the Pyramus
    story is "the only one which was not in some way ludicrous." Thomp-
    son (*Shakespeare's Chaucer*, p. 93), suggests that it is ludicrous.
18 Brian Gibbons, editor of the new Arden edition of *Romeo and Juliet*
    (London: Methuen, 1980), p. 31, notes that *Romeo* and *The Dream*
    "must have been written very close together" but ventures no priority;
    a census of editions shows a slight editorial preference for supposing
    the priority of *The Dream*. Muir (*Sources*, p. 77) suggests as one of the
    purposes of the Pyramus play Shakespeare's wish "to show intelligent
    members of the audience that *Romeo and Juliet*, written about the same
    time, was an unsatisfactory tragedy because it depended too much on
    a series of accidents." One supposes that Shakespeare would allow in-
    telligent members of the audience to draw their own conclusions; he
    may, however, have been cheerfully acknowledging his own awareness
    that his tragedy was melodramatic in the extreme.
19 The translation is that of N. E. Griffin and A. B. Myrick, eds., *The
    Filostrato of Giovanni Boccaccio* (Philadelphia: University of Pennsylvania
    Press, 1929), p. 347. The Italian reads, "E tu, per cui tanto il dolar mi
    serra, / E che dal corpo l'anima divelli, / Ricevimi, Criseida volea
    dire."
20 Quotations from *Romeo and Juliet* are from the edition introduced by
    Frank Kermode in *The Riverside Shakespeare*.
21 In my approach to this scene I am indebted to Louis L. Martz's lecture
    on the play, delivered at Indiana University in the spring of 1980, of
    which he was kind enough to send me a copy; if the reader finds any-
    thing offensive in what I say, the fault is entirely my own.
22 *The Riverside Shakespeare*, p. 1057.

Chapter 2

1 For the range and history of the acknowledgments, see Thompson,
   Shakespeare's Chaucer, pp. 88–94. Her own discussion is surprisingly
   brief. Harold Brooks observes (in the new Arden edition *Dream*, p. lix)
   that Shakespeare's debts to Chaucer are "greater and more significant
   than Ann Thompson indicates," and Brooks's own notes and introduction contain far more references to Chaucer than any previous edition
   of the play.
2 Bethurum, "Shakespeare's Comment on Mediaeval Romance," pp. 85–
   94. As her title indicates, Bethurum is primarily interested in the play's

use and abuse of a literary form and a literary tradition, whereas I am concerned with its handling of romantic attitudes.

3 Jan Kott, *Shakespeare Our Contemporary*, trans. Boleslaw Taborski (London: Methuen, 1965), pp. 171–90. Kott seems to believe that the lovers copulate during their stay in the woods, and the same suggestion is occasionally made by other critics: I can find no support for it in the text. Kott's emphasis on the "bestiality" of Titania's love for Bottom seems to ignore the fact that Bottom is an ass in head only.

4 That the play was written to celebrate a wedding is a conjecture that has gained wide acceptance. Brooks puts the case for it succinctly: "Grant the presumption, and it accounts for the inclusion and clarifies the relevance of everything in the play. Reject it, and there can still be no doubt that love in relation to marriage is the dramatist's subject," (*Dream*, p. lxxxix). I certainly agree that the subject is love in relation to marriage, but then the subject of most romantic comedy is love in relation to marriage. There are elements in the play that the conjecture does not account for without a good deal of forcing. I refer especially to the characters of Oberon and Theseus and their spouses, who have to be made into various kinds of matrimonial role models in order to fit the conjecture and who do not seem to me to be up to playing the parts critics assign them.

5 C. L. Barber, *Shakespeare's Festive Comedy* (Princeton: Princeton University Press, 1959), p. 140. Barber's discussion of the play's skepticism is excellent, especially with regard to the role of the fairies.

6 Samuel Johnson, "Preface to Shakespeare." The critical urge to moralize *A Midsummer Night's Dream* is very strong, and the literature is full of attempts that often cancel out other attempts.

7 Bethurum, "Shakespeare's Comment," p. 91.

8 Brooks quotes Nevill Coghill to this effect (ed., *Dream*, p. lxxix, n. 1).

9 Perhaps the most drastic critical attempt to make Theseus a moral mentor, and Oberon another, is Paul A. Olson's article, "*A Midsummer Night's Dream* and the Meaning of Court Marriage," *ELH*, 24 (1957), 95–119. Theseus' and Oberon's inconvenient amours are reduced to a single sentence in a discussion of Oberon: "Like Theseus, he may have wandered in the mazes of love and war, but, again like Theseus, he has overcome these" (p. 109). Olson sees Theseus as embodying "the reasonable man and the ideal ruler of both his lower nature and his subjects" (p. 101). For the pre-Shakespearean development of this Theseus, Olson cites Natalis Conté, Arthur Golding, Sir John Davies, and Alexander Ross, but rather neglects Shakespeare's immediate source, North's Plutarch, who is much preoccupied with Theseus' womanizing. Brooks points out (ed., *Dream*, p. lxxix) that North does reinforce the Chaucerian idea of Theseus as a good ruler, but adds that Theseus' amours as described by North make him "the reverse of a patron of marriage."

10 Brooks, ed., p. ciii.

11 To do so would be to emphasize in Oberon a petty jealousy ill-becoming a patron of marriage.

12 Olson, however ("Court Marriage," p. 102), remedies Shakespeare's failure to consider Titania's amorous past by labeling her a threat to "the fixed hierarchy of wedlock."

13 The influence of *The Knight's Tale* on *The Two Gentlemen of Verona* is noted by Clifford Leech in the new Arden edition of the play (London: Methuen, 1969), p. xxxvi; see also Bullough, *Narrative and Dramatic Sources*, I, 203.

14 This motif appears, of course, in other works that influenced Shakespeare's play, notably Lyly's *Endimion*.

15 See III.ii.195–219. The characters of the two women, combined with the relative shallowness of their husbands-to-be, seem another impediment to an interpretation of the play such as Olson's and, less dogmatically, Brooks's, as an allegory showing marriage to be the triumph of the male reason over the female passion or flesh. Lysander and Demetrius are singularly devoid of reason.

16 Olson suggests ("Court Marriage", p. 108) that Pluto and Proserpina are analogous to Theseus and Hippolyta, "the higher realities," whereas May and January, like the lesser lovers in the play, are "their imperfect copies." This seems a curious use of the words *higher* and *imperfect*: a perfect copy of Pluto and Proserpina would seem to me to rate very low on any scale of reality.

17 Brooks, ed., *Dream*, p. cvi. With unfailing honesty, Brooks acknowledges (p. cvii) that Oberon is a rather fallible mentor, and concludes that he is "obviously not a perfect being." But Brooks's defense of him proceeds largely by derogation of Titania, and even Titania is made guilty by association. Brooks's footnote, p. cvi, n. 2, says of Titania "that she is to be judged as a rebel wife, the parallel with Hippolyta directs." Brooks cites James L. Calderwood, "*A Midsummer Night's Dream*: The Illusion of Drama," *MLQ*, 26 (1965), 511, and Olson ("Court Marriage", p. 99) to establish Hippolyta's status as a rebel wife, on which Titania's is made to depend. But there is absolutely nothing in *A Midsummer Night's Dream* to suggest that Hippolyta was a rebel woman whom it was morally necessary for Theseus to subdue. The passage the scholars depend on is from *The Two Noble Kinsmen* (I.i.83–86) and concerns a wholly different Hippolyta and Theseus. One begins to feel that the scholars are putting together a new play from other or non-Shakespearean sources.

18 Brooks cites Calderwood ("Illusion of Drama," p. 511) in support of his statement that it was high time the Indian boy be taught to become a knight and huntsman. Calderwood accuses Titania of "violating natural order" "by refusing to let the boy pass from a feminine into a masculine world where, if natural growth is to have its way, he belongs." Calderwood cites Barber (*Festive Comedy*, p. 137), who says parenthetically that the Indian boy, released by Titania, "now goes

from her bower to the man's world of Oberon." But Oberon says that the boy has now gone to *his* bower in fairyland (IV.i.60), where Oberon has said he will serve as Oberon's "henchman" (II.i.121). That Oberon is interested in the child's education depends solely on Puck's remark that "jealous Oberon" would have him "knight of his train, to trace the forests wild" (II.i.24–5).

19 It is not clear whether Oberon is jealous because Titania is so devoted to the boy or because she has the boy.

20 Calderwood ("Illusion of Drama," p. 512) faces down this issue squarely by announcing that the words show that "Oberon sets about restoring order."

21 Cf. Olson ("Court Marriage," p. 109), "Shakespeare's king of Shadows is also a delicate figure for grace. He is the play's Prospero." Oberon's imprecision in instructing Puck into whose eyes to put the distillation makes him a figure for Inefficient Grace.

22 It seems immaterial at what point Shakespeare combined Robin Goodfellow and Puck: the former is the mischief-maker of folklore, whereas the latter has something of the Devil's dignity.

23 Kott, *Shakespeare Our Contemporary*, p. 171.

24 In *Huon de Burdeux*, from which Shakespeare took the name Oberon, the fairy king is benevolent to Huon alone, rescuing him again and again, and always forgiving him for disobeying orders—not only, as Olson suggests ("Court Marriage," p. 108), when Huon is "sinless or penitent." Oberon in *Huon* is a good old-fashioned otherworld fairy whose motives are simply not open to analysis by residents of this world. He is not a Christian.

25 See *Sources and Analogues of Chaucer's Canterbury Tales*, pp. 343–47. Seeing what occurs, St. Peter asks the Lord to make the husband blind again.

26 Cf. Calderwood, "Illusion of Drama," p. 521: "Suggestions that beneath the surface of ordered, civilized, rational existence lies a gulf of meaninglessness and even latent malignity—'jaws of darkness' in wait for true love—are certainly present, but they are triply distanced from the audience, which sees them as created by Shakespeare's play, by Puck's and Oberon's magic 'play,' and by the dream-play of the lovers' own minds." The first part of this sentence seems to me a splendid summary of the spirit of the play; and if the second part means that the dark suggestions do not spoil our pleasure in the play, I wholeheartedly agree; but if what is meant is that the suggestions are there but we must not see them, my disagreement is total.

27 Bethurum, "Shakespeare's Comment," p. 88.

Chapter 3

1 Edwards, "On the Design of *The Two Noble Kinsmen*," pp. 89–105. See p. 94: "It seems to me that Shakespeare was fired by the dark Chaucer-

ian vision of what happened to two men [Palamon and Arcite] pursu-
ing their desires, or being pursued by their desires."

2 Thompson, *Shakespeare's Chaucer*, pp. 166–215. Thompson makes an
exhaustive, scene-by-scene comparison of the play with the poem.

3 Leech, ed., *The Two Noble Kinsmen*.

4 I have compared Leech's apportionment (ibid., p. xxiv) with that of
Hallett Smith in his edition of the play in *The Riverside Shakespeare* (p.
1640), and that of Thompson (*Shakespeare's Chaucer*, p. 167), as well as
that of G. R. Proudfoot in his edition of the play (Lincoln: University
of Nebraska Press, 1970), p. xvi. It appears that Shakespeare is generally agreed to have written I.i–v (with some uncertainty about iv–v),
II.i (some uncertainty), III.i, V.i, iii–iv; Fletcher is generally assigned
the remainder, though III.ii is sometimes given to Shakespeare, as are
IV.ii–iii. Most of the uncertain scenes concern the plot of the jailer's
daughter, which I do not discuss. For what it is worth, my own ear
agrees with the common opinion; for reasons explained below, n. 13,
it seems to me impossible that IV.ii could be Shakespearean.

5 Cf. Edwards, "Design," pp. 93–94: "The Knight's Tale is a magnificent
study of human helplessness, of men and women floundering after
happiness, but, being entirely at the mercy of love, of the mighty of
the world, and of the gods—or destiny—or fortune, moving steadily
into wretchedness."

6 The disagreeable aspects of the temple of Venus in *The Knight's Tale*
have often been ignored by Chaucerians: Edwards (ibid., p. 93) takes
them fully into account.

7 Quotations from the play are from the edition introduced by Hallett
Smith in *The Riverside Shakespeare*. This passage is quoted by Theodore
Spencer, "*The Two Noble Kinsmen*," *MP*, 36 (1939), 271, as "a dignified
and exalted piece of writing," but it seems to me that its dignity hardly
compensates for its gruesomeness. For the Elizabethan belief in the
value of war as a purge, see Kenneth Muir, *Shakespeare as Collaborator*
(London: Methuen, 1960), p. 138.

8 See I.iv.4–5; pointed out by Thompson, *Shakespeare's Chaucer*, p. 202.
Quotations from Chaucer are from Speght's 1602 edition.

9 Edwards, "Design," p. 99.

10 Ibid., pp. 103–04.

11 Leech, *The Two Noble Kinsmen*, p. xxx. I feel that Edwards underrates
the force of Emilia's speech (as Hippolyta tries to) when ("Design," p.
98) he speaks of "Emilia in childish love with Flavina," and that he is
going beyond the text when (p. 97) he calls Flavina's and Emilia's love
one "of absolute spontaneity and absolute innocence."

12 "Design," p. 94.

13 Proudfoot, (ed., *The Two Noble Kinsmen*, p. xvi) lists this scene as one
about which doubt has been expressed, but the impression it gives of
Emilia is so much at variance with her earlier and later Shakespearean
appearances as to make Shakespeare's authorship of it impossible. I

conjecture that Fletcher patterned it loosely after Emilia's later appearance when she considers the worth of the two knights while they are fighting (V.iii).

14 I.iv is listed as questionably Shakespeare's by Leech, p. xxiv, and by Smith, p. 1640, but is listed without question as Shakespeare's by Thompson, *Shakespeare's Chaucer*, p. 167, and by Proudfoot, p. xvi.

15 The death of the losers is first proposed by Theseus in III.vi, a scene written by Fletcher, but there is no diminution of his bloodthirstiness in Act V, in scenes written by Shakespeare.

16 Edwards "Design," p. 104.

Chapter 4

1 Quotations from the play are from the edition in *The Riverside Shakespeare*.

2 Quotations from Chaucer are from Speght's edition of 1598; but since Shakespeare may have had an older copy, I have compared Speght's text with Stow's (1561) and Thynne's (1532), but have found no startling differences. The play was apparently written in 1601–02 before the appearance of Speght's 1602 edition, which is in any case very similar to that of 1598. In the passage quoted, modern editions read "leste" for "moste" in line 281 and "meuynge" for "meaning" in line 285. See the discussion below.

3 J. J. Jusserand's judgment that "Shakespeare seems never to have read Chaucer's admirable version of the story" is quoted in the New Variorum edition of *Troilus and Cressida*, ed. H. N. Hillebrand (Philadelphia: Lippincott, 1953), p. 448. The editor himself observes (p. 449) that "if Sh. read Chaucer he did so rather casually, borrowing remarkably little, and giving nowhere evidence of that careful attention which he was wont to employ" with other sources. Some scholars, though admitting that Chaucer's poem was a source for Shakespeare, believe that he could not have understood it very well: see, e.g., n. 6 below.

4 John Bayley, "Time and the Trojans," *EIC*, 25 (1975), 68. In an earlier discussion, Bayley had wondered whether the two women "are not in fact almost the same woman": "Shakespeare's Only Play," *Stratford Papers on Shakespeare 1963*, ed. B. W. Jackson (Toronto: W. J. Gage), p. 79.

5 See n. 2 above. The editions of 1542 and 1550 are textually close to Thynne's 1532 edition.

6 In *Shakespeare's Troilus and Cressida and Its Setting* (Cambridge: Harvard University Press, 1964), p. 27, Robert Kimbrough writes, "But even if he [Shakespeare] read Chaucer's *Troilus and Criseyde* it was with a double handicap: he never knew Chaucer as a deft manipulator of metrics, rhyme, and diction, and he knew *Troilus* with Henryson's *Testament of Cresseid* appended. . . . I should think that many subtleties of characterization and interior monologue would have been lost to

Shakespeare because of the controverting influence on Chaucer's narrative of the 'epilogue' full of diseases and divine retribution."

7 Heider Rollins, "The Troilus-Cressida Story from Chaucer to Shakespeare," *PMLA*, 32 (1917), 426. Rollins was following a suggestion
made by J. S. P. Tatlock: see Tatlock's edition of the play in the Tudor
Shakespeare (New York: Macmillan, 1912), pp. xviii–xix. Rollins' article had enormous influence on the criticism of Shakespeare's play.

8 The authoritative text of Denton Fox, ed., *The Poems of Robert Henryson* (Oxford: Clarendon Press, 1981), reads "worthy" for black-letter
"lusty."

9 For "forged" Fox's text reads "fenȝeit."

10 Modern editions read "eighthe" for black-letter "seuenth."

11 I feel that Shakespeare's literary intelligence was such that, if he had
seen it, he would have been able to resist the implication of the head-
note prefixed to *Troilus* in Speght's 1602 edition: there the reader is told
that the poem relates Criseyde's "great vntrouth" in yielding to
Diomede, "who in the end did so cast her off, that she came to great
miserie." In 1599, Francis Thynne in his *Animadversions* on Speght's
edition of 1598 recognized *The Testament* as non-Chaucerian.

12 That Cressida's bad character was so firmly established by Shakespeare's time that he could not have changed it is the chief purport of
Rollins's article. Earlier, R. A. Small, *The Stage Quarrel between Ben
Jonson and the So-Called Poetasters* (Breslau, 1899), p. 156, had observed
that in Shakespeare's day "a treatment of the story so palliative of Cressida's character as was Chaucer's would have been impossible." For the
persistence of the idea see W. W. Lawrence, "Troilus, Cressida, and
Thersites," *MLR*, 37 (1942), 425, where he remarks that, if Shakespeare had altered for the better the character of Cressida, "his audience
would have been bewildered, and his play wrecked."

13 A browse through the criticism of the play is on the whole a disheart-
ening experience for one who has affection for Cressida. Among the
sterner judges of her (of whom there are many) is Albert Gerard, *ES*,
40 (1959), 146: as a "connoisseur of lust, well-acquainted with the niceties of the game of love, she is the worthy niece of the go-between
Pandar, with whom she exchanges jokes in somewhat questionable
taste." Others damn her no less pointedly if less moralistically for frivolity and shallowness: see, e.g., A. P. Rossiter, *Angel with Horns*, ed.
Graham Storey (London: Longmans, 1961), p. 132: "She is a chatty,
vulgar little piece, and in the rhyming soliloquy at the end [of I.ii]
(where she speaks what she takes for her mind), the principles of the
loftily chaste heroines of *amour courtois* are brought down exactly to the
level of Mrs. Peachum's advice in *The Beggar's Opera*." Occasionally
she is allowed enough depth for love despite her shallowness: thus Clifford Leech, "Shakespeare's Greeks," *Stratford Papers on Shakespeare
1963*, p. 11: "Cressida is faithless, but she is alive and witty. Her love is
shallow and it can be a bit cheap, as when she reproaches Troilus for

leaving her early in the morning after they have become lovers. . . . But that her feeling is rightly to be called 'love' can, I think, hardly be questioned." Her wit seems sometimes to be taken as an indication of her shallowness: see E. M. W. Tillyard, *Shakespeare's Problem Plays* (Toronto: University of Toronto Press, 1950: rpt. 1954), p. 54: Cressida by "her mechanically witty interruptions [of Pandarus] shows herself as an efficient society woman without depth of feeling." Coghill, *Shakespeare's Professional Skills*, p. 107, sees shallowness from a slightly different perspective: Shakespeare imagined Cressida "as a chameleon-girl, who takes moral colour from whoever she happens to be with [*sic*]; she responds at once to every environment." Hamill Kenny, "Shakespeare's Cressida," *Anglia*, 61 (1937), defends her but finds her "selfish" and "frail" (p. 169), with "small self-knowledge" (p. 174).

One of the earliest of her defenders, John Palmer, is quoted in the New Variorum edition of the play, p. 554, as thinking her "one of the loveliest of Shakespeare's tragic figures." Her most formidable defender of the past generation of Shakespeareans was Tucker Brooke, "Shakespeare's Study in Culture and Anarchy," *The Yale Review*, 17 (1928), rpt. in *Essays on Shakespeare and Other Elizabethans* (New Haven: Yale University Press, 1948); Brooke calls her, p. 73, "a flower growing in Trojan slime, a little soiled from the first and shrinkingly conscious of her predestined pollution." Emphasis on Cressida's condition as victim induces sympathy for her, but also tends to drain the force out of her personality and diminish her ability to interest us. Thus Gayle Greene in *The Woman's Part: Feminine Criticism of Shakespeare*, ed. C. R. S. Lenz, G. Greene, and C. T. Neely (Urbana: University of Illinois Press, 1980), pp. 133–49, and Barbara H. C. de Mendonça (de Almeida), "*Troilus and Cressida*: Romantic Love Revisited," *SQ*, 15 (1964), 327–32, both justly show her as victim but leave little in her to admire.

Cressida's ambiguity, which I stress, naturally leads to highly divergent reactions to her among the critics, and sometimes to changes of mind. The best example of this is Robert K. Presson, whose Harvard dissertation is cited in the New Variorum, p. 421, as believing that "the elevation of Cressida's character which Shakespeare achieved . . . is the best indication of the great debt Shakespeare owed to Chaucer"; but in its published form, *Shakespeare's Troilus and Cressida & the Legends of Troy* (Madison: University of Wisconsin Press, 1953), Presson's opinion of Cressida seems to be summed up by his remark on p. 132 that Shakespeare pictures her throughout as a prostitute.

Ralph Berry, *The Shakespearean Metaphor* (London and Basingstoke: Macmillan, 1978; rpt. 1980), p. 122, n. 4, justly remarks that the "rehabilitation of Cressida marks a groundswell of modern criticism." He cites for special notice Joseph Papp, "Directing *Troilus and Cressida*," *The Festival Shakespeare Troilus and Cressida* (New York, 1967), pp. 23–72. Another eloquent recent defense of Cressida is that of R. A. Yoder,

"'Sons and Daughters of the Game': An Essay on Shakespeare's *Troilus and Cressida,*" *ShS,* 25 (1972), 11–25; this contains a splendidly fair-minded analysis of the relationship of Troilus and Cressida. The best straightforward defense of Cressida of which I am aware is that of M. M. Burns, "*Troilus and Cressida*: The Worst of Both Worlds," *ShakS,* 13 (1980), 108–30. This fine article has anticipated in print a number of the points I make in this and the next chapter. I am sorry that Burns's study was not available before I completed the earlier form of my own that was published in *Poetic Traditions of the English Renaissance,* ed. Maynard Mack and George deF. Lord (New Haven: Yale University Press, 1982), p. 67–83.

14 Of the many comparisons of the two women the one most damaging to Cressida is that of Muriel C. Bradbrook, "What Shakespeare Did to Chaucer's *Troilus and Criseyde,*" *SQ,* 9 (1958), 311–19. F. S. Boas, *Shakespere and His Predecessors* (New York, 1896; rpt. New York: Greenwood Press, 1969), p. 375, finds Shakespeare's the worst of all Cressidas, "a scheming coldblooded profligate" compared to the "charming coquette of Benoît, the voluptuous court-lady of Boccaccio, the tender-hearted widow of Chaucer."

15 For an excellent history of the Cressida-figure in the Middle Ages, see Gretchen Mieszkowski, "The Reputation of Criseyde 1155–1500," *Transactions of the Connecticut Academy of Arts and Sciences,* 43 (1971), 71–153.

16 Philip Edwards, *Shakespeare and the Confines of Art* (London: Methuen, 1968), remarks, p. 103, that the "play constantly tells us of inconstancy."

17 Since the conception of Criseyde on which this study is based is my own and varies greatly from that held by most Shakespeareans, I repeat here material that has been much more fully presented elsewhere: "Troilus and Criseide," in my *Chaucer's Poetry: An Anthology for the Modern Reader,* 2d ed. (New York: Ronald Press, 1975), pp. 1129–44; "The Masculine Narrator and Four Women of Style" and "Criseide and Her Narrator," in *Speaking of Chaucer* (London: Athlone Press, 1970), pp. 46–83; "Chaucer and the Elusion of Clarity," *E&S* (1972), pp. 23–44; "Briseis, Briseida, Criseyde, Cresseid, Cressid: Progress of a Heroine," in *Chaucerian Problems and Perspectives,* ed. Edward Vasta and Zacharias P. Thundy (Notre Dame: University of Notre Dame Press, 1979), pp. 3–12; "Chaucer in the Twentieth Century," *Studies in the Age of Chaucer* 2 (1980), 7–13. In *Shakespeare's Chaucer,* pp. 121–27, Ann Thompson shows a shade more sympathy for Cressida and less for Criseyde than is customary, but still seems to me rather prejudiced in her responses. Thompson makes many of the comparisons I do, though usually with different emphases and to different effect.

18 Modern editions read "and allone, / Of any frend to whom she dorste hir mone." The introduction of Criseyde is a fine example of what Alice S. Miskimin suggests is the narrator's role, "to shield and filter

the action as it unfolds in retrospect": see *The Renaissance Chaucer* (New Haven: Yale University Press, 1975), p. 219.

19 The classic statement of Criseyde-suspicion is that of A. S. Cook, "The Character of Criseyde," *PMLA*, 22 (1907), 531–47; see also R. K. Root, *The Poetry of Chaucer* (Boston: Houghton Mifflin, 1906), pp. 107–13. In recent years condemnation has become rather rare, and Criseyde is treated more tenderly than she deserves.

20 Donaldson, "Chaucer in the Twentieth Century," p. 10.

21 John Bayley "Time and the Trojans," p. 68.

22 At III.iii.20–22 Calchas tells the Greeks, "Oft have you (often have you thanks therefore) / Desir'd my Cressid in right great exchange /Whom Troy hath still denied."

23 Hamill Kenny ("Shakespeare's Cressida," p. 170) observes that Cressida "loved Troilus at first sight: Cressida, then, was more easily enamored" than Criseyde. It is not wholly logical to suppose that falling in love at first sight is a sign that one is easily enamored: a woman may have resisted a hundred attractive suitors before being suddenly enamored of one. Comparing the two heroines, one might well find it more shocking to witness Chaucer's Criseyde falling in love with great deliberation with one man through two and a half books and then falling in love with another in less than half a book than to see Cressida violently in love with one man at the very beginning of the play and falling in love with another at the very end. But to fall in love at first sight calls forth the disapproval of moralists: Virgil K. Whitaker, *Shakespeare's Use of Learning* (San Marino: The Huntington Library, 1953), p. 211, says that Cressida's falling in love at first sight "was contrary to Christian ethics and psychology," and adds, p. 213, that when "next" Shakespeare portrayed "genuine and worthy love, he made absolutely clear that it had not come at first sight."

24 Burns ("Worst of Both Worlds," p. 106) acutely observes how the "name-calling" that is so characteristic of the play has infected critics: "the voice which pronounces the word 'whore' in real-world criticism of the play testifies to the contagion of that aggression which the play portrays."

25 See *Shaw on Shakespeare*, ed. Edwin Wilson (New York: Dutton, 1961), pp. 194–95.

26 I apologize to readers of my essay on Criseyde-Cressida in *Poetic Traditions of the English Renaissance* for giving on p. 74 figures that, because of what I can only call idiotic inadvertence, left out a whole scene in which Cressida figures prominently.

27 Cf. Burns, ("Worst of Both Worlds," p. 107), who observes that Cressida's questions in I.ii show that she "notices the people and events around her" and "takes an interest in people as people."

28 Eric Partridge, *Shakespeare's Bawdy*, revised ed. (New York: Dutton, 1969). A scene involving Hero, Beatrice, and Margaret, discussed by

Partridge on pp. 31–32, seems to me to be the high-water mark of feminine bawdiness in Shakespeare.

29 See the note to the line in *The Riverside Shakespeare*.

30 Kenneth Muir in the Oxford Shakespeare edition (Oxford: Clarendon Press, 1982) and Kenneth Palmer in the new Arden edition (London: Methuen, 1982) see nothing in the line to annotate.

31 K. Deighton, ed., *Troilus and Cressida* (Indianapolis: Bobbs-Merrill, 1906), n. to I.ii. 277–79 (256–57 in *Riverside*).

32 Kenneth Palmer (new Arden ed.), pp. 116–17, nn. to 261 and 262, seems to suggest that a "minc'd man" whose "date is out" is impotent, but the only evidence he adduces is Pandarus' reply, which he apparently feels recognizes an obscenity, though he does not say how.

33 Johnson was bothered by the poor logic of "wiles" being defended by "wit," and suggested that "will" should be read for "wiles." Almost all the editions I have consulted gloss the hard or unusual words but fail to address the general sense, beyond noting that Cressida is speaking with irony and obscenity. In his Pelican edition, Virgil K. Whitaker (Baltimore: Penguin Books, 1970) merely notes that the "passage fully establishes Cressida's moral level." Kenneth Palmer does make an effort to explain Cressida's sense, but his conviction that every word she says must have a secondary sexual meaning heightens the impression of obscenity without much clarifying the sense.

34 *As You Like It*, III.ii.204.

35 See the fine discussion of this passage in Burns, "Worst of Both Worlds," pp. 109–10. Burns concludes: "Obviously, a woman cannot defend her belly by lying on her back, nor can Cressida depend on Pandarus to defend her; this entire speech relates solely that, in fact, Cressida has no defenses. In order to deal with the world in which she lives, she must needs be 'at a thousand watches'."

36 Bradbrook, "What Shakespeare Did to Chaucer's *Troilus and Criseyde*," p. 314. See also Rossiter's condemnation of Cressida's soliloquy, n. 13 above. Burns ("Worst of Both Worlds," pp. 110–11) finds the speech an expression of Cressida's vulnerability, and asks sensibly whether "Cressida could be said to gain some material or emotional benefit from holding out against Troilus."

37 See the Textual Notes to I.ii.287, 290, and 294 in *The Riverside Shakespeare*, p. 492.

38 Thompson (*Shakespeare's Chaucer*, p. 119) remarks that the "fear that Pandarus attributes to Cressida . . . seems no more than an affected parody of Criseyde's genuine and characteristic apprehension ('Right as an aspes leef she gan to quake,' iii.1200)." I have noted above the double image the narrator gives of Criseyde, first coolly administering first aid to her fainting lover and then quaking in his embrace. There is actually more reason to suspect Criseyde's quaking to be role-playing than there is to suspect Cressida's panting.

39 Ernest C. Pettet, *Shakespeare and the Romance Tradition* (London: Staples

Press, 1949), p. 149, condemns Cressida's explanation for "its insincerity, pretence of innocence, calculation, and provocative coquetry."

40 See, e.g., Boas, *Shakespere and His Predecessors*, p. 375: Cressida "affects a fear that, in her rapture, she will betray her emotions too unreservedly, and with an ambiguous request to stop her mouth, she draws him into kissing her."

41 Muir in the Oxford edition, p. 32, remarks that "Cressida's confession of love and her admission that she has concealed her feelings show that she has become infected with Troilus's sincerity. . . ." (Cf. Coghill's "chameleon-girl.") It is uncertain whether Pettet allows Cressida even borrowed sincerity.

42 J. Oates Smith, "Essence and Existence in Shakespeare's *Troilus and Cressida*, PQ, 46 (1967), 179. Troilus is speaking prose.

43 Arnold Stein, "*Troilus and Cressida*: The Disjunctive Imagination," *ELH*, 36 (1969), p. 149. I am uncertain whether Stein thinks Cressida is consciously provoking jokes, or whether he thinks she is merely responding to the needs of her psyche.

Chapter 5

1 See Troilus' conversation with Pandarus at IV 540–81, and specifically 563–67, where he says that any open attempt to keep Criseyde in Troy would disclose their relationship and bring slander to her name.

2 See IV 603–04 where Pandarus assures Troilus that Troilus could make peace with Criseyde easily if she were angry at his having kidnapped her.

3 At IV 636–37 Troilus tells Pandarus he will not kidnap her without her permission, and in the following stanzas Pandarus promises to arrange a meeting of the lovers during which Troilus can ascertain what Criseyde's wishes are in this respect.

4 Troilus makes this suggestion twice, at IV 1506–26 and 1601.

5 See Criseyde's soliloquy at V 736–40.

6 The admiration of critics for Shakespeare's Troilus tends to increase with their lack of admiration for Cressida. With the exception of a few who, like O. J. Campbell, *Comicall Satyre and Shakespeare's Troilus and Cressida* (San Marino: The Huntington Library, 1938), p. 212, consider him a lustful roué, the more conservative critics tend to take him on Ulysses' valuation (IV.v.96–112) and consider him an idealist brought down by his love for an immoral woman. See, e.g., Mary Ellen Rickey, "'Twixt the Dangerous Shores': *Troilus and Cressida* Again," *SQ*, 15 (1964), 10: "Cressida's worthlessness forces Troilus into steady decline from a near-perfect suitor and soldier to a weak and divided man"; see also Tillyard, *Shakespeare's Problem Plays*, pp. 79–80. Troilus' reputation has deteriorated as Cressida's has improved. Muir in the Oxford edition (p. 31) illustrates the nice balance that is often made between esteem of one and disesteem of the other: Troilus "is depicted

as young and inexperienced; and although it would be unfair to say that he regards Cressida merely as a sex-object, he is deluded by her appearance to credit her with imaginary virtues." But where Cressida's character is praised Troilus' conversely tends to be damned. For an excellently judicious account of both the lovers see R. A. Yoder, "Sons and Daughters of the Game." See also the next two notes.

7 The remarkable exclusion of Cressida as a person from this speech has been noted by David Kaula, "Will and Reason in *Troilus and Cressida*," *SQ*, 12 (1961) 275.

8 Joyce Carol Oates is so taken with Troilus' poetry that she credits him with speaking it when in fact he is speaking prose: see Chapter 4, n. 42, and the text to which it refers.

9 Verity's explanation, apparently preferred by the Variorum, p. 158, as well as by Palmer and Muir, suggests that Cressida really was angling for Troilus' thoughts and then realized that he was too wise not to see that she was, and hence perverts the proverb. But this is both too prejudicial to Cressida—she seems more likely to be suggesting that if she had been angling for his thoughts he was too wise to be caught—and also fails really to solve the non-sequitur. It seems to me that she is both trying to credit Troilus with wisdom and to assure herself that he loves her, though she does so characteristically with an open-ended statement that could allow that he does not love her.

10 See *OED*, But, *prep.*, *conj.*, *adv.*, 25. Burns ("Worst of Both Worlds," p. 112) observes that Troilus' speech "virtually forbids Cressida's constancy."

11 The curious exchange between Troilus and Cressida at III.ii.61–75 seems to suggest both lovers' consciousness of a mismatch, but especially Cressida's. See her remark that she sees "in the fountain" of their love "more dregs than water"—though it is Troilus who had introduced the image by asking her "what too curious dregs" she saw in the fountain of their love. Cf. Burns, "Worst of Both Worlds," pp. 119–20.

12 See Fox's edition of *The Testament*, lines 546–74. The line quoted occurs at 546 and 553, and, with slight variation, at 560.

13 The line was first thus emended by Hanmer in 1744.

14 The omnipresence in the bedroom of Chaucer's Pandarus is emphasized not only by his coming to the rescue when Troilus faints, stripping off his outer garments, and casting him into the bed (III 1093–99), but also by his highly self-conscious retirement with the candle to the fireplace (1135–42), and finally, by his (?unheard) remark to Troilus that if he is wise, he will not swoon again (1188–90); this last occurs after the lovers have reconciled and, because our interest is in them, after we have forgotten all about Pandarus, who with this remark "laid him to sleep."

15 See "Chaucer's Three 'P's': Pandarus, Pardoner, and Poet," *MQR*, 14 (1975), 284–85 and 294–95, for a fuller discussion of Pandarus' behavior with Criseyde. Comparing the Shakespearean and Chaucerian

scenes, Thompson (*Shakespeare's Chaucer*, pp. 133–34) remarks that Shakespeare's version "is coarsened by the lack of innocence or honesty on the part of Cressida," and though noting a number of details that Shakespeare borrows from Chaucer, she observes that "it is basically a similar situation altered by a different appraisal of the characters, especially the heroines. Both are complex, but Criseyde's complexity lies more in her creator's subtle portrayal of what is really a straightforward and simple character, while Cressida has a personal complexity which is simultaneously sophisticated and crude." This comes very close to saying that Criseyde is an optical illusion who, if she were to become real, would become Cressida. The only substantive difference that Thompson sees between the two women is that Cressida lacks innocence and honesty, and this charge is either not true or, if it is true, is equally true of Criseyde. The critic seems guilty of trying to make a sense of good taste into a moral principle.

16 Thompson (*Shakespeare's Chaucer*, p. 125) notes that "in Chaucer as well as in Shakespeare 'honour' is an ambiguous concept, . . . a matter of mere appearances," and that "stripped of her author's sympathy, Criseyde is little better than Cressida in this respect. . . ." Criseyde's preoccupation with honor is well illustrated at IV 1576–82. It should perhaps be noted that both in Chaucer's and Shakespeare's time, it was the woman who earned dishonor through an illicit love affair, not her lover.

17 At IV 667–68 Chaucer's narrator informs us that, compared with her love for Troilus, Criseyde cared nothing for her father, nor when he died.

18 See the discussion in Chapter I.

19 As Muir notes in the Oxford edition of the play, p. 142, n. 106, Cressida's non-Chaucerian "clear" voice occurs in Henryson's description of Cresseid: it is mentioned in *The Testament*, in lines 176, 338, and 443.

20 In considering Troilus' remarkable failure to consider how to prevent Cressida's departure, Yoder, "'Sons and Daughters of the Game',", p. 21, asks us to imagine "Romeo or Hamlet in his place—would they be tamed to this hollow, passionless performance?" Troilus's failure to take action is also noted by de Mendonça (de Almeida), ("Romantic Love Revisited," p. 331).

21 That Ulysses' judgment of Diomed calls into question his competence as a judge of character has been noted by G. L. Voth and O. H. Evans, "Cressida and the World of the Play," *ShakS*, 8 (1975), 239, n. 12.

22 Of course a director can cause the actor playing Cressida to perform in such a way as to confirm what Ulysses says, but it is nevertheless amazing that so many astute critics have not troubled to compare what Ulysses says about her with what Shakespeare's text presents her as doing. A. S. Knowland, for instance ("*Troilus and Cressida*," *SQ*, 10 (1959), 357) thinks that we cannot eradicate from our knowledge of

Cressida as she appears in speech, gesture and movement, the impression, which she is surely intended to create, of shallowness and frivolity, of weakness," and so forth. The critic is describing not the text but a given performance of the play. Cf. Tillyard, *Shakespeare's Problem Plays*, p. 75: Ulysses "sees through Cressida instantly, while the other Greek leaders make fools of themselves"; Carolyn Asp, "Th'Expense of Spirit in a Waste of Shame," *SQ*, 22 (1971), 356: "Once she [Cressida] reaches the camp of the 'merry Greeks' her clever wit and wanton spirits gain the ascendency, and she engages in a round of raillery and kissing with the Greek generals." In 1937, Hamill Kenny ("Shakespeare's Cressida," p. 168) noted of Cressida that "seven of the Greeks greeted her before she said a word!" But many critics thereafter have ignored her silence in order to hear, with Ulysses, her body's speech.

23 F1 reads "tickling" for Q "ticklish": either reading seems satisfactory, though I feel that that of F1 is perhaps pithier; Ulysses himself, however, seems ticklish rather than tickling. Burns ("Worst of Both Worlds," p. 124) has a fine discussion of the fallaciousness of Ulysses' condemnation of Cressida.

24 The text's "a coasting" seems no more than a spelling for Elizabethan and modern "accosting," which makes perfect sense.

25 Whether Shakespeare understood the black-letter "not" for the "noot" that Chaucer probably wrote is not clear: Modern English "not" is often spelled "nat" in the early printings of Chaucer, but by no means uniformly. But many readers (and even some scholars) have failed to realize that the narrator is saying that he does not *know* whether Criseyde gave Diomede her heart rather than he does *not* say she did, and such readers have missed only a slightly richer irony.

26 This is an echo of a remark that the narrator makes when Criseyde first thinks of accepting Troilus as her "servant" and the narrator is anxious to dispel the notion that she fell in love with him too quickly: first, he says, she began to incline to like him, and then his manliness and his suffering made love "mine" within her, "For which by processe and by good seruice / He wanne her loue and in no sodain wise" (II 678–79). Having thus slowed down the process, the narrator in the next stanza speeds it up when he tells us that in any case the planet Venus was at that time so situated as to help Troilus in his love, and that, as a matter of fact, Venus was not altogether a foe at his nativity, so that he succeeded the sooner! The process is reversed in Book V, where Criseyde's love for Diomede is first speeded up and then belatedly slowed down.

27 The passage that Shakespeare had in mind when he was writing Lorenzo's speech in *The Merchant of Venice* (V.i.1–6) occurs in Chaucer earlier, in the ten-day waiting period at 666–79.

28 See n. 26 above.

29 Brooke, "Shakespeare's Study in Culture and Anarchy," p. 74.

Chapter 6

1 Thompson, *Shakespeare's Chaucer*, p. 109.

2 Ibid., p. 95.

3 Brooke's text is taken from Bullough, *Narrative and Dramatic Sources*, I, 284–88. The bracketed word "to" appears as "the" in the original.

4 P. 98. Quotations from Chaucer are from the edition of 1561; the Shakespeare is from *The Riverside*.

5 As Bonnie Wheeler points out, "Dante, Chaucer, and the Ending of *Troilus and Criseyde*," *PQ*, 61 (1982), p. 110, Troilus' eventual destination, to which Mercury leads him from the seventh/eighth sphere, "is hidden from our knowledge." For further discussion of Troilus' ultimate domicile, see Elizabeth Kirk, "'Paradis Stood Formed in Hire Yen': Courtly Love and Chaucer's Re-Vision of Dante," *Acts of Interpretation: The Text in Its Contexts 700–1600*, ed. Mary J. Carruthers and Elizabeth D. Kirk (Norman: Pilgrim Books, 1982), pp. 257–77. I should perhaps say here that my understanding of Chaucer's poem and that of D. W. Robertson, Jr. (see especially "Chaucerian Tragedy," *ELH*, 19 (1952), 1–37) are so far removed from one another that we seem to lack any common ground on which we might profitably argue.

6 See, e.g., John Gardner, *The Life and Times of Chaucer* (New York: Knopf, 1977), p. 215. Responsibility for the mistake is probably in part C. S. Lewis', who, in *The Allegory of Love*, so stresses the importance of adultery to courtly love and of courtly love ideas to *Troilus and Criseyde*, that one is almost forced to find adultery in it.

7 See Donaldson, "The Ending of Troilus," *Speaking of Chaucer*, pp. 84–101.

8 A number of similarities between the two characters have of course been noted in the criticism, but no actual influence of Chaucer on Shakespeare's concept of Falstaff has been shown. Ann Thompson (*Shakespeare's Chaucer*, p. 83) speaks rather scornfully of "the attempts of some critics to draw comparisons between such figures as Falstaff and the Wife of Bath as 'rich comic characters'," on the uncertain grounds that Shakespeare "seems to have thought of Chaucer *primarily* as a writer of romantic and courtly poetry rather than as a comic naturalist" (p. 82). But this is to allow a preconception to override any evidence the text may provide to the contrary. In "The Non-Comic, Non-Tragic Wife: Chaucer's Alys as Sociopath," *ChauR*, 12 (1978), 171, Donald Sands disallows all comparison between Falstaff and the Wife of Bath by announcing, "There is no abysm of evil in him, and such an abysm may exist in Alys." Against moralization so self-assured and so prejudiced neither the Wife of Bath nor literature itself has any defense. Perhaps the best reply to Sands is to quote an equally surprising statement by Nevill Coghill—here pulled rudely out of context but not falsifying his opinion: "Chaucer had no vision of evil": see *Elizabethan and Jacobean Studies Presented to F. P. Wilson*, p. 99.

9 See *Piers Plowman by William Langland: An Edition of the C-Text*, ed. Derek Pearsall (Berkeley and Los Angeles: University of California Press, 1978), Passus V, lines 32–57.

10 Judith J. Kollmann, "Ther is noon oother incubus but he: *The Canterbury Tales, Merry Wives of Windsor* and Falstaff," in *Chaucerian Shakespeare: Adaptation and Transformation*, ed. E. T. Donaldson and J. J. Kollmann ([Detroit:] Michigan Consortium for Medieval and Early Modern Studies, 1983), pp. 43–68.

11 See my "Designing a Camel; or, Generalizing the Middle Ages," *TSL*, 22 (1977), 1–16, for a fuller discussion of Jerome's misinterpretation.

12 *King Henry V*, II.iii.9–26. Despite its brilliance, I find Theobald's famous emendation of F1 "Table" to "babbl'd" too emotive, and prefer the conjectural emendation "talk'd." The bracketed words near the end of the passage are in Q1–3, and seem to me to have been left out of F1 through scribal error.

Index

Scholars referred to only in the notes are listed if they are quoted or their opinions discussed. Fictional characters of Chaucer and Shakespeare who are extensively compared in the text are given separate entries rather than being listed under the works in which they appear.

Index

The Swan at the Well

Shakespeare Reading Chaucer

E. TALBOT DONALDSON

While critics have long acknowledged the literary connection between Shakespeare and Chaucer, most take for granted the simplicity of Chaucer's works and assume that Shakespeare did so as well. In this witty and learned book, a deeply experienced interpreter of Chaucer points out some of the great subtlety and multiplicity of meanings of Chaucer's poems and argues that Shakespeare perceived that complexity and often reflected it in his reworking of Chaucerian material.

E. Talbot Donaldson here focuses on the Shakespearian plays and figures most indebted to Chaucer. He considers, for example, that *Troilus and Criseyde* and *Romeo and Juliet* are both magnificent if sad celebrations of romantic love, and that Falstaff and the Wife of Bath are triumphant if unsavory celebrations of human vitality. He discusses the influence of four Chaucerian works — most especially *The Knight's Tale* and *The Tale of Sir Thopas* — on *A Midsummer Night's Dream*. Probing the relation of Shakespeare's *Troilus and Cressida* to Chaucer's poem about the lovers, he demonstrates the similarity of the two poets' basic approach to their heroines, and shows how in this case a misreading of Chaucer may result in a misreading of Shakespeare.